THE TALES CHRIST TOLD

THE TALES
CHRIST TOLD

by

April Oursler Armstrong

ST. BEDE'S PUBLICATIONS
Petersham, Massachusetts

St. Bede's Publications, Petersham, Massachusetts 01366

Printed in the United States of America

97   96   95   94   93   92   91   90   5   4   3   2   1

Library of Congress Cataloging-in-Publication Data

Armstrong, April Oursler
   The tales Christ told / by April Oursler Armstrong.
      p.   cm.
   Reprint. Originally published: Garden City, N.Y. : Doubleday,
1959.
   ISBN 0-932506-82-8
   1. Jesus Christ--Parables. I. Title.
   BT375.2.A7   1990
   226.8'09505--dc20
                                                    90-34304
                                                      CIP

To my daughter Clare:

who someday will suddenly feel
that His tales are all true
in His love!

AUTHOR'S NOTE

How does a book come to be written?

It begins with an awareness. This book began with an afternoon's conversation, when the Italian-born Rev. Peter Mongiano, I.M.C., fired a wintry sullen day with his own intense interest in the parables. It was spurred into progress by the literary enthusiasm of an English friend whom I have yet to meet in person, Mr. R. J. O'Connell.

I could not begin to name all those whose encouragement and help in the research and reconstruction of these tales nursed this manuscript to completion. But I want to thank especially the Most Rev. Thomas J. McDonnell, D.D., Coadjutor Bishop of Wheeling; Rev. John de Marchi, I.M.C.; Rev. Marius McAuliffe, O.F.M.; Mr. Edward Aswell; Mr. Ralph Beebe; Mr. William Berger; Mrs. Frank Jerabek; Mr. Neil McCaffrey—and my own smilingly patient family.

CONTENTS

INTRODUCTION

A strange man-made wall stands today around the Bible. Our Scriptures are printed on elegantly thin paper, gold-leafed, fragile. An air of somber remoteness envelops every word. And many have the unconscious impression that Christ's words somehow float in mid-air, held aloft by angels. They forget that Jesus Christ, Son of God, was also Son of Man. He was of earth as well as of heaven.

When He preached in the countryside of Palestine nearly two thousand years ago He was speaking to men and women of all time—to Peter and James, to Mary and Martha, but also to you and to me. And we must learn how best to hear Him.

He spoke most often in the story form we call the parable. He would take things of everyday life—yeast in the bread dough, lost money, a runaway son—and use them to spell out eternal truth.

A parable is, really, as the original Greek word says, a comparison. It is not a fable. It is not an allegory, in which words are used figuratively. A parable places two things together so that we may see the likeness—and, incidentally, overlook the difference.

Jesus did not invent the parable. There are parables in the Old Testament and some in the rabbinic literature of the

Jews. But Jesus used them as no one else has, with the authority of one who is Master of both the earthly and the divine.

Why did He use parables? Partly to make truth plain, partly to cloak it in mystery.

He used parables to make truth plain because His listeners were mostly plain folk, then and now. Few of us feel at home juggling the giant abstractions of life and death, salvation, predestination, grace and free will. We do feel at ease with things we can see and touch, with the divine patterns we see at work here on earth. And when Jesus captures the vast heavens in the pocket mirror of human earthly life we can understand.

But He also used parables to obscure the truth. He would at times interpret the parables only to His disciples and leave the rest of His audience to make what they could of them.

Why was this? Certainly the explanations of the parables were not to be kept secret forever. The explanations He gave to His disciples are in the Bible now for everyone to read. It was for His immediate audience, then and there in Palestine, that obscurity was needed.

For one thing, the Jews of the time had many wrong notions of what the Messiah would be and do, often expecting the Christ to be a rebel leader, a political figure rather than a spiritual Savior. And Christ, when He spoke of His kingdom, was most careful to speak in parables, feeding the faith of those who sought the spiritual, discouraging those who looked for an earthly kingdom.

We were meant to understand the parables, we who belong to His kingdom. The trouble today is that, though the obscurity of those times is gone, new obscurities have risen to rob us of the parables' soul impact. There is a veil of language and of changed customs, so that we no longer under-

stand the meaning of a guest's wedding garment, of foot washing, of a shepherd's place in religion.

And there is, too, the sad fact that many of us live cut off from the earth, encased in brick and concrete and iron fencing. We do not know the ways of seed and seedlings, or of sheep, the struggle against drought and weed and wolf and storm. And so we lose the intimate meaning of His teaching.

Our parables today would be of busses and pickpockets, perhaps, of evening newspapers and cups of coffee, of window boxes instead of fields. But such parables would not last. They would have to be remade for our children in terms of rockets and jet engines, of interplanetary space and housekeeping problems on a satellite.

Christ told His parables in terms of the things that never change, in the barest fundamentals of living. And we can claim them for our own if we will make the effort to pierce the years with a little study, to breathe the clean air of the countryside and lift our eyes to the stars.

It is good for us to take the evergreen branches of the parables in our hands and look on them with new eyes, till the memory of the heft and odor of them clings to us and perfumes the air we breathe.

For these are truly His tales of life—of life on earth, and of life eternal.

THE TALES CHRIST TOLD

1

THE SOWER AND THE SEED*

Hᴇ sᴛᴏᴏᴅ in the sun on the hillside. His face, young in His thirty years, golden in the light, was earth-plain. He was a man among men, cleanly but poorly dressed, with the strong stance of one used to walking. Only His eyes set Him apart. As someone once said, they were His Father's eyes.

Around Him, near the Lake of Genesareth, men and women sat listening in the still spring noontide. They had left their work, left shops and markets in towns, left fields and beasts, when they heard He was here. They came to listen. And, as so often, He was telling them a story, the strange kind of story called a parable.

"The sower went out to sow his seed. . . ."

The men squatting in the fields nodded. Only a few weeks before, in the months we would call January and February, which in that gentler land are the time of the planting of summer grain, all through the countryside men had gone out to sow seed. Not a man listening this morning to Him did not know the weight of the sack of seed, the cool slippery feel of it in his hands as he sent it over the earth, the rhythm of the sowing.

"And as he sowed, some fell by the wayside . . ."

* Matthew 13:1–23; Mark 4:3–9; Luke 8:5–18.

The fields of Palestine were small, odd-shaped, carved by trees and paths and the intricate family transactions of the past. And seed was scattered by hand. Only the most valuable seeds such as barley were laid out singly in rows. For the rest, a man strewed it broadside. And seed did fall on the edges of the dusty roads, sometimes traveling with a breeze far out into the paths. Everyone knew that.

"And it was trodden down, and the birds of the air devoured it."

The men grinned. Who had not heard the crows descending on his field? The partridge and quail, the wild pigeons fed on the wasted seed.

"And other seed fell on a rock, and as soon as it had sprung up it withered away, because it had no moisture."

Rock! The men grunted. Half the fields were rock, gray with stones like the refuse of creation, underlaid with hidden ledges. You could not plow most of this land. And if you dug out the rocks one spring, more came to light with each new rain. The seed that fell on the thin earth above the rocks germinated and sprouted and then died when the roots struck the ledge. You need deep rich earth to grow a crop.

"And other seed fell among thorns, and the thorns, growing up with it, choked it."

The men sighed. Brambles infested the ground like a disease, spreading and flourishing the minute a man turned his back. There were thorn plants and thorn trees, thistles and briers and nettles, and father and son and his son's son would work to remove them, and there would always be more to choke the crop.

"And other seed fell on good ground and, springing up, yielded fruit a hundredfold."

The men nodded with satisfaction. Already the fields were green with the promise of harvest from the seed that was saved. So it had always been. So it would always be, praise heaven.

Then suddenly the voice of Jesus ripped like thunder through the spell of that simple story.

"He that has ears to hear—let him hear!"

And they knew that once again He had taken the simple green-smelling homely parts of their lives and given them new meaning. The sower, the seed, the rocks—all these were to speak to them of the things of God. A parable this was, a way of talking where things had double meaning, a picture story of eternal truth.

The crowd stirred and rustled. It was for the parables that they loved to hear Jesus speak. They were not abstract thinkers, these men and women, not intellectuals. They were used to dealing with what they could see and touch. And they knew that the One God Who made all things could use the humblest parts of His creation to show forth His truth to men.

Slowly, in groups of five and six, the men left, carrying with them the music of His voice and a thought they could ponder each day of life.

What did it mean, this recital of the facts of seeding a field?

The disciples asked Him that. And gently He explained: "The seed is the word of God."

And the seed that falls by the wayside is like the people who hear the word of God and do not particularly believe it or receive it into themselves. And then the devil comes like the flock of crows and takes the word of God out of their hearts. And they are not saved.

The seed that falls on the rocks and springs up only to wither is like the people who hear the word of God and become excited about it and believe it for a while—while life runs smoothly. Then, in the strong sun of temptation, they give up, for the roots of their faith are not deep enough to sustain them. And they are lost.

The seed that falls among thorns is like those who hear the word of God and believe but who are choked and strangled by the cares and riches and delights of life. They are not strong enough to pierce through these things, and their faith bears no fruit and is useless.

"But that seed on the good ground are those who in a good and perfect heart, hearing the word, keep it and bring forth fruit in patience."

Christ Himself is the sower. The seed is the word of God. The sower is skilled, and spreads the seed evenly over all. The seed is good and, given a chance, it will grow and blossom forever. The problem is in the ground, in the one who receives it. For not everyone who hears the word of God and begins to live with it will be saved.

It was the perfect parable for men of the land. So long as men anywhere in any time seeded a harvest they could meditate on those words. A day at work in the fields was a page from God's own catechism, thanks to that parable. Over the centuries the tale of the sower would become part of the texture of thought and language of all men.

Were He talking today to modern city folk He might have used a different example. No one can say what He would have said. But studying the parable of the sower, turning it over in our minds and hearts, it is good sometimes to think of what in our day might tell the same truth.

Today, for example, we might imagine some vast well-organized emergency health measure. Suppose an epidemic threatened our city, a deadly disease for which one prolonged regime of medication held prevention and cure. We can imagine that a packet of that medicine with a letter of detailed instructions for the months ahead is sent to every address in the city.

Some would throw it away unopened, to litter the streets and be trodden underfoot and swept up by street cleaners. Some would open it, read it with fair interest, put it in the To-Be-Done file, and forget it. Some would read it and follow directions till the taste of the medicine gagged them and the novelty of danger palled. Some would really mean to keep on but the pressures of their social calendar would eat up their time, and their budgets would lean more to sweets than medicine, and they too would give up.

And some would receive the medicine and message, follow it no matter what the cost, patiently, earnestly, and triumphantly. They would survive the epidemic. The others would not.

The medicine was infallible. Everyone had a chance to take it. And not everyone did. Their fate was in their own hands. And so, of course, is ours. The word of God comes to us all. It is up to us to see that we receive it well.

There are parallels to the sower and the seed in all that we do today, far from fields and rocks and weeds. An advertiser mails a broadside barrage of literature and expects at best a ten per cent response. A teacher gives all she can, knowing that only a few of her pupils will rise to the challenge of real learning. A woman practices kindness to everyone she meets, knowing that only a few will give kindness, even a smile, in return.

And yet the parable told that day by the lake cannot be bettered. For it was of the earth as God made it, in tune with the eternal mysteries of life and death. The seed of life was in each word.

In a city park in London, in the sprawling mechanized farms of the American Middle West, in a backyard garden or a window box there is still seed and a sower—a promise to be fulfilled or thwarted.

As the green season quickens the earth and winds carry the hint of God's new glory into city streets, we, like the men of Galilee, may ponder. Are we an open highway to the traffic of the world, too busy with other thoughts to take the word into ourselves at all? Are we stonehearted, too cynical, too proud to receive the life of faith and hold it through the hot sun of life? Are the brambles of worry and greed reaching out to choke our faith and keep it earth-bound, before it can bear fruit in sacrifice and self-denial? Or are we good soil, where faith roots deep?

"He that has ears to hear, let him hear."

And He left the hillside, walking ahead of the disciples, His eyes caressing the rock-strewn field and the blue-gray lake—the Sower patiently tending His harvest.

2

THE GOOD SAMARITAN*

He was the simplest person who ever lived. And that was what confused the intelligentsia.

In people's minds, the more hopelessly complicated a thing is the more important it is. A genius is expected to have at least nine neuroses. An idea is not considered profound unless it's so cluttered with big words that no one can understand it. We decorate thoughts and things and people with dust catchers and camouflage—and then we are impressed.

He was totally unadorned. He wore plain clothes. He used plain speech. He lived and laughed and suffered with the absolute economy of a single blade piercing the earth to grow and bloom and ripen. Even His joy was gaunt and strong, singlehearted.

He was the richest personality the world has known, perfectly integrated. His teaching is the eternal deep truth—yet it seems simpler than a child's fairy tale. Just as one simple ray of white light contains every known shade of color, so the truth of Christ contains the answer to every question of man's soul.

The trouble is that men—whose minds can never be big enough to enfold the truth of the God Who made them—find

* Luke 10:30–37.

it hard to be simple when they talk about God. And, sadly, they can get so interested in talking about God in big words and fancy discussions that they lose sight of Him completely. That happens today. And that is what had happened to the religion of Israel by the time Jesus came to earth.

The Scribes and the Pharisees knew all about religion, and very little about loving and serving God. They were, as Jesus told them, so busy about the letter of the Law that they killed the spirit of it. He was so disgusted with them that He called them a bunch of whitewashed coffins—dainty outside, full of corruption and worms inside.

And they, in turn, were horrified by Jesus. He was in their eyes a religious ignoramus, an unholy boor, and a blasphemer. He was—too simple. And they became His thoroughly complicated bitter enemies.

But one Scribe came to Jesus, an honest intelligent man with a simple question—the only question worth asking:

"Master, what must I do to possess eternal life?"

Now a Scribe, though not a priest, was a qualified expert in divine law. He was a judge and a teacher, competent to tell men what was right and wrong in God's eyes. And the law of God had become extraordinarily complicated—thanks to the work of centuries of self-important complicated men. There were three hundred positive commands and three hundred negative commands to be obeyed if you wanted to please the Lord—a bramble of rules to confuse a simple soul.

This Scribe knew them all. It was his career to know the precise rules for making sacrifice, for cleaning dishes, for protecting orphans, for tithing mint and cumin crops, and so on. But this Scribe was looking for something beyond the rules, some one principle to give meaning to the whole Law. He was looking for the simple truth.

And the question flew like a flaming arrow from the heart of man to the heart of Jesus:

"What must I do to possess eternal life?"

Jesus turned, His eyes searching the Scribe's earnest face. "What is written in the Law?" He said. "Tell Me, how do you read it?"

The Scribe stepped closer, drawn by that gentle voice. He answered with words from the Book of Deuteronomy, words every good Jew repeated twice a day in the ritual prayer of the Shema:

"Thou shalt love the Lord thy God with thy whole heart, and with thy whole soul, and with all thy strength, and with all thy mind——"

And then, taking a breath, he added words from another part of Scripture, from the Book of Leviticus: "*—and thy neighbor as thyself!*"

And, hearing that, Jesus smiled and stretched His arms out as if in greeting. The first law everyone knew—so well that they had practically forgotten to listen to its meaning. But the second law, the love of neighbor, was not the kind most Pharisees and Scribes stressed.

Jesus said: "You have answered rightly. Do this, and you shall have everlasting life."

Do this, He was saying, *and you will find you have obeyed every law God has made. The laws are complicated because men require them to be. The Ten Commandments are only another way of saying: "Love God and your neighbor." Moral theology is only the detailed textbook of case histories in the science of that love!*

"Love!" is a command like "Live!" To live, your body must fulfill a million small rules—but you do not think of all the rules unless you are a physician, or in need of one. To love, you must obey a million small commands of duty and service

—but you need not focus on the commands if you have learned to love.

The Scribe felt his heart swell as if quickened with new life. But one question remained, the one that would pierce the curtain of the Pharisees forever.

"And who," whispered the Scribe, "who is my neighbor?" Whom must I love, Master?

The Pharisees teach that only Pharisees are worthy of the love of God or of other men. No one but they can hope to qualify for this exclusive club of heaven. But, Master, You have taught men to pray, calling God our Father—and You have taught that prayer to all men.

Is it to be so simple? Love *everyone* and love God? Are we all to be one—Jew and Samaritan and Gentile and pagan? Is that the key to truth?

Jesus answered with a parable never equaled, the tale of the good Samaritan.

"A certain man," He said, "went down from Jerusalem to Jericho—and he fell among robbers."

The Scribe, and the crowd gathered around him, knew the scene well. The road down the mountains from Jerusalem to the edge of the Jordan was famous for its danger. Bandits lurked in the hills and barely a day passed without some news of terror reaching the city.

Jesus continued: "They stripped him, and wounded him, and went away, leaving him half dead.

"And it happened that a certain priest went down the same way and, seeing him, passed by. And also a Levite, when he was near the place and saw him, passed by."

A priest. And a Levite—who was by birth a helper in the Temple, a singer at services, a servant of priests, somewhat like a deacon. They should have stopped. And yet, thought the people listening, who could blame them? Even children were taught to be wary of strangers. And a man lying naked and moaning by the road was quite likely to be a decoy for a bandit's trap. You might stop to help someone and end up a victim yourself. Or the man might be drunk, or crazy, and not hurt at all. At any rate, you ran the risk of getting involved in a long complicated mess by stopping. The priest and the Levite would be in a hurry, on official business, no doubt. . . .

Even today the most proper and religious people are likely to cross the street rather than pass too close to a man slumped in a dark sidewalk corner. Even today, rather than get involved as a police witness, men and women hurry past an accident case, consoling themselves with the thought that someone else will take care of it. . . .

"But," said Jesus, the whisper of a smile teasing in His eyes, "a certain Samaritan, being on his journey, came near him and, seeing him, was moved with compassion."

A Samaritan? His audience sat up straight on their heels. A Samaritan was an unspeakable outcast, lowest of the low. All Jews hated the men of Samaria as a matter of course. It was not race prejudice, for Samaritans were Jewish and they too had received the law of Moses. But in the long twisted history since Sinai they had split off from the men of Israel in politics and in religion. And the Jews considered Samaritans traitors and heretics, unclean, and a disgrace to God and to the chosen people.

For Jesus to choose a Samaritan was like waving an orange flag on St. Patrick's Day—or making a hero out of a Nazi storm trooper.

But He continued calmly: "The Samaritan went to the man and bandaged his wounds, pouring on oil and wine. And putting him on his own beast, he brought him to an inn and took care of him. And the next day he took out two days' wages and gave them to the innkeeper and said: 'Take care of him, and whatever you spend over and above this I will repay you when I return.'"

Jesus paused, His glance challenging the startled faces around Him, resting finally on the quiet face of the Scribe, who alone seemed to understand.

"Which of these three, in your opinion," asked Jesus, "was neighbor to the man that fell among thieves?"

"The one who showed mercy to him," whispered the Scribe.

Jesus nodded gravely. "Then go—and do you in like manner."

Go—and treat all men as your neighbor. Love all men as you love yourself and God, not counting cost, not weighing gain. The Samaritan was in a hurry too. He too had prudent reason to be afraid. He gave up time and money and safety without hope of reward, without asking who the victim was. The Samaritan, whom the Pharisees scorn, pleased God because he understood how to love his fellow man.

It was as simple as that. Love God. Love all men. For all now are one in God.

Do that and you will live. For love is the spirit of the living God, by Whom and in Whom we all live.

It was not the kind of religion that appealed to the Pharisees then or now. But it was and is the truth.

The laws of God are many, and real. We do need a code of morality to guide and discipline us. But we must not turn the code into a false god by itself. The one law that matters is the law of love. It is the beginning and end of all others.

"For God so loved the world, that He gave His only begotten Son . . ."

3

THE PRODIGAL SON*

H E W A S not what the Pharisees considered proper at all. He was not careful of His company. He mingled in the most unsavory crowds. And He seemed to have no awareness of or respect for the social and religious lines between one group and another. Stubbornly, deliberately, He spent hours talking not to the professors of religion but to heaven's outcasts. It was, the Pharisees agreed, a scandalous way to behave, demoralizing to the whole system of society.

Everyone knew that the Pharisees alone kept the law of God in all its written and oral complications. Everyone knew that only in Jerusalem, only under the guidance of scholars, could a Jew hope to please God. But this Jesus was out in the hinterlands preaching. He did not ask if a man were clean or unclean. He *preferred* to talk to sinners. That was the crux of it. He stood with them in the market places, in the fields. He even went to their houses and ate with them. And He spoke to them in a tone they had not heard before—a voice so tender that even the hardest soul listened.

He stood now, His cloak flung back over His shoulders, a smile tugging at His deep eyes. At the edges of the crowd around Him the Pharisees had been talking among them-

* Luke 15:11–32.

selves. They had seen Him speak kindly to a man who they knew had not made sacrifice in the Temple in seven years. They had heard Him greet a publican, one of the despised tax farmers whose moneygrubbing oppressed the poor and served the Roman occupation forces. And behind their sleeves the Pharisees had sneered in horror at this Master Who received sinners.

The crowd had heard them. He had heard them too. And in answer He told a parable, a tale never surpassed, never forgotten.

"A certain man had two sons," Jesus began. "And the younger son said to his father: 'Father, give me my share in your estate now.' So he divided his property between his two sons. And not many days after, the younger son, gathering together all that he owned, went abroad into a far country."

The men listening tugged at their beards. A son so impatient for his inheritance showed little love for his father! It took an amazingly patient man to overlook this sin against filial piety and give him his inheritance at all!

"And there," Jesus continued, "he squandered his fortune in riotous living.

"And after he had spent all his fortune, there came a mighty famine in that country, and he found himself in want. And he went and attached himself to a citizen of that country—who sent him to his farm to feed swine!"

The men grinned. A Jew in a pigsty—with pigs the most unclean of animals named under the Law! It was the height of indignity. But such a son deserved what he got. He insulted his father, he went into Gentile land, he spent himself recklessly in sin. . . .

"He would have been glad to fill his belly with the husks the swine ate," said Jesus. "But no man gave him even that to eat.

"And then he came to himself and said: 'How many hired servants in my father's house have more bread than they can eat, and here I am perishing with hunger! I will arise and go to my father and say to him, Father, I have sinned against heaven and before you; I am not worthy to be called your son; make me like one of your hired servants!'"

Jesus paused. The men listening nodded with sad half-smiles. Easy enough to repent a sin in misery! Who did not? But who would welcome back such a son, prodigal, reckless in throwing away not only money but a father's love and God's good pleasure?

His father would have mourned him as dead, if not in body at least before God's law. He had broken every commandment. He was not fit to be even a servant in a good man's house.

But the voice of Jesus continued:

"And he arose and went on his way to his father.

"And when he was still a great way off his father saw him and was moved with compassion and, running to him, he threw his arms around him and kissed him!

"And the son said: 'Father, I have sinned against heaven and before you. I am not worthy to be called your son.'

"But the father said to his servants: 'Bring the best robe and put it on him. And put a ring on his hand. And shoes on his feet. And bring out the calf we have been fattening, and kill it. Let us eat and make merry. For this my son was dead and is come to life again. He was lost, and is found!' And they began to make merry."

Jesus smiled. This was not the ending they expected. He held them in strange silence, the stunning scene of forgiveness beyond belief. He continued, His voice nimble in the web of narrative, spinning the picture before their mind's eye:

"Now the elder son was out in the fields. And as he came back to the house he heard music and dancing. And he called one of the servants and asked him what this meant.

"The servant said: 'Your brother has come home, and your father has killed the fattened calf because he has him back safe!'

"And the elder son was angry and would not go in.

"His father came out to talk to him. And he said to his father: 'Look how many years I have served you, and I have never defied your commands, and yet you have never given me even a kid to feast on with my friends. But as soon as this son of yours comes, a son that has eaten up his inheritance with harlots—you have killed for him a fattened calf!'"

The men shifted in their places and eyed Jesus closely. Who could blame the elder brother? There was no justice in this reckless forgiveness! Why, you could even say the father was more prodigal than the son—prodigal with love at any rate. Could this be what Jesus was teaching?

Jesus continued:

"The father said to the elder son: 'Son, you are always with me. And all I have is yours. But'"—and here the voice of Jesus rose with new force, vibrant with meaning—"'but it was right that we should make merry and be glad. Your brother was dead, and has come to life again. He was lost and he is found!'"

And in the silence Jesus raised His deep eyes to the Pharisees who stood on the edges of the crowd.

What did it mean, this parable of two sons and a father?

Those who heard Him that day understood. It was a story of their own lives, and of the Father Who is God—a story that explained why this Jesus came to sinners.

It was a story of love, of the Father Who never forgot the son who had left Him. The Father watched for him every day. And when, in the depth of misery, he had realized the terrible meaning of sin and come humbly home, the Father had not waited for him to crawl abjectly before Him. The Father had come running to embrace His son!

That was the love of God, beyond justice, beyond reason, a love that hungered for the return of a sinner.

The good were His already. The good had His love. But they were not to be self-righteous, not jealous of their position in His eyes. They were to love with His own love—to yearn as He does for the return of their wandering brothers.

God is the real spendthrift, Jesus was saying, and the treasure of His mercy and love is inexhaustible.

And men pondering that tale found with a smile that it carried a two-edged point.

To the sinner, the younger son, it gave hope, the amazing promise of the Father's forgiveness. He had only to come back, only to start on the way to Him, and He would catch him up in His love.

But to the good man, to the elder son, it gave warning. There must be no smugness in the good, no resentment. The elder son must rejoice with the Father, or he will exclude himself from the feast and the merrymaking. If he refuses to love the sinner as the Father does, he will find himself out in the cold, "refusing to go in."

On that day when Jesus spoke, as so often since, the sinners heard and understood, and the Pharisees heard and did not wish to understand.

The parable of the prodigal son would be told and retold through the centuries, always with a certain sense of wonderment. Men would find it was a story that needed no revision, as new and real today as it was in the time of Jesus. There are always reckless spoiled young men plunging selfishly into sin, waking up when it is almost too late. There are always the good earnest souls who do keep the rules and work hard, and expect their reward.

But men through the ages would find that it was really quite difficult to tell the story exactly as Jesus did. It is human nature to try to slip in a sermon, a scolding from the father to the son, a rebuke before the embrace. Try telling that story to a child someday, and see for yourself. No human being can forgive so completely, so unreservedly, as the Father.

And, telling it, you will realize that only God Himself could fashion such a parable. It is a story not of human forgiveness but of divine love and mercy. And the difference between the two is the banner of our hope of heaven.

On that day Jesus stood with love in His eyes, His arms spread to embrace all the sons of the Father, the elder and the younger. And some turned to meet that embrace. And some did not.

It was, they said, a story almost too good to believe.

And so, of course, is God's love almost beyond belief.

4

WOLVES IN SHEEP'S CLOTHING*

Some teachers, many of them, talk about truth. But Jesus was Truth, talking. And that made the difference.

When He spoke men listened.

It is not easy to listen to anyone without interruption. To listen for hours to a discourse on the nature of God and of man, of good and evil, and the purpose and proper manner of life, is more than the average man can bear.

But on the mountain slope beyond Capharnaum more than a hundred ordinary men had sat listening to Jesus while half a day's shadows crossed the lake below. Later they would search for words to say what set Him apart from other teachers. He taught with authority, they would say, with power—not as the Scribes and Pharisees.

Still, He was not what is known as a spellbinder. Listening, you did not fall into a trance of admiration, to waken later in exhaustion and pleasant confusion. You were, if anything, more alive as you listened, as if His words carried energy to quicken the soul.

These men around Him were not scholars. A few years of the public school in the synagogue, a short apprenticeship at a trade, was all that prepared them for life. Yet it was to them

* Matthew 7:13–20.

Jesus addressed that mountain sermon, the first course ever given in Christianity.

What He put into words was the very spirit of Himself, the eternal truth, simple because it was as much a part of Him as breath. And as men who cannot cope with chemical valences still delight in fresh water, in air and the green of plants, so the fishermen and tradesmen and hired hands on that slope caught and held the first touch of Christianity.

He stood in His hand-woven tunic, a turban on His long hair, with a rough gray rock as a pulpit. He seemed rooted in that mountain, as if for all time He had been here, teaching. Yet His face was young, as full of life as the wild flowers that played in the wind.

He had begun by laying down a startling set of qualifications for the holiness of Christians. They would be poor in spirit, and meek. They would mourn, and hunger and thirst after justice. Merciful, clean of heart, peacemakers they would be. For the sake of Him they would suffer persecution and be reviled. And their reward would be heaven itself, for they would be the children of God.

One by one He took the commandments, like some new, younger, stronger Moses, and held them so that they shone with fresh fire. He had not come to destroy the old law of God, He said. Who could destroy truth? But He had come to fulfill it with new meaning. He had come to insist that men live the law in a broad tide of love, surging beyond the limits of words.

He spoke to command men to be perfect—as their Father in heaven is perfect.

"Love!" He said. Love everyone, and love God, trusting, setting your heart on the kingdom of heaven, sacrificing, working, suffering, being certain that God watches over you.

From anyone else those words would have been pleasant piety, the impracticality of a young daydreamer.

But these were no dreams. They were the stuff of His soul, the essence of this Man on the mountain. And, listening, every soul there knew that Jesus of Nazareth would live and die in this truth.

He did not pretend it would be easy. He did not promise anything on earth, except suffering and humiliation and temptation and trial—and the constant tender fatherly love of God.

The Twelve, whom only this morning He had finally chosen as His own, listened soberly to these marching orders for the conquest of the kingdom of heaven. Each one by itself was a small shock, an affront to human nature. *Turn the other cheek. . . .* Peter shifted on his haunches. *Lay not up treasures on earth. . . .* Matthew spread his hands on his knees.

Jesus was demanding the denial of all that men took for granted, the contradiction of all earthly desires. And He asked instead that men seek the will of God.

It was impossible. But, seeing Him there, men sensed that in Him the impossible had been done. Framed against earth and heaven, He seemed to live with a deeper, wider, higher life in which all things were possible—a life where God and man became one.

He promised them heaven. And not a person in that wind-swept silence doubted that He could and would keep that promise.

It would not be easy. The gate of heaven was narrow, He said, and the road precise and difficult. There were other roads a man could choose—broader, easier ones, the kind you can walk with your eyes on the passing sights. But there was only one road to eternal life, only one of truth.

"And"—His voice seemed to catch with sudden sorrow—
"how few there are who find it!"

He leaned forward on the rock, His eyes darkening in
pleading.

"Beware of false prophets," He said. He had laid the course
clear, pointed the way. Later His spokesmen would guide
His followers farther along the road. But others would speak
who were not of the truth. . . .

"Beware of false prophets, who come to you in sheep's
clothing—but inwardly they are ravening wolves!"

A *wolf in sheep's clothing*—it was a phrase that had become
part of folklore, even here in Israel. Five hundred years before, Aesop had told in Egypt a fable of a wolf that dressed
itself in the skin of the sheep it killed, and of the motherless
lamb that followed that wolf to destruction. And the tale had
not been new with Aesop. . . .

The voice of Jesus now was like the voice of a father arming
his sons with wisdom for the day they would go out into the
world—urgent, tender in its warning, hoping against hope to
save them from deception and peril.

And for His followers, the flock whom He would teach to
know Him as the Good Shepherd, that phrase had a new and
haunting impact.

He was the voice of truth, the way, and the life. But there
would come among His flock men of falsehood, masquerad-
ing in the dress of holiness to destroy the life of His sheep.
Hypocrites and heretics there would be, luring the lambs
with the outward show of Christianity, drawing them away
from the path of righteousness to death.

John and James, the two nearest to Jesus, raised their eyes
in question. How was a man to know a false prophet? How
could you look beneath the skin to see the truth?

"By their fruits you shall know them," He said. "Do men

gather grapes from thornbushes, or figs from thistles? Even so every good tree produces good fruit, and the evil tree produces evil fruit. A good tree cannot produce evil fruit, nor can an evil tree bring forth good fruit."

Around Him men nodded. There was, after all, only one way to tell the worth of anything, and that was by the fruit of it, the completion. Weeds produce weeds. Vines yield grapes. A rotten tree betrays itself in misshapen, scanty fruit. And a man is known by his deeds. Words can be a mask to hide the inner spirit, but the substance of a man is in the way he lives—and dies.

"Every tree," said Jesus, "that does not produce good fruit shall be cut down and shall be cast into the fire! Therefore, by their fruits you shall know them."

Cast into the fire—as a tree falls when the good farmer detects its rotten core, so the deceivers would fall and be destroyed!

And then, as if to be certain they understood, as if to press into their hearts the everlasting awareness of danger, He said:

"Not everyone who says to me: 'Lord! Lord!' shall enter into the kingdom of heaven.

"But he who does the will of My Father Who is in heaven —*he* shall enter into the kingdom of heaven!"

Till the end of time men would remember that warning. A man may call himself a Christian and wear the name of Christ like a mantle and still be cast into the fire. Before Jesus Himself died one of these Twelve who called Him Lord would meet that judgment. While Peter still lived the first hypocrites would move into the fold with the sheep. The world would find each new generation spawning its own deceivers.

Some there would be who posed as holy men, loyal to God's

law, divinely appointed spokesmen to lead men to new truth. And inwardly they would carry only death, beckoning, panicking the flock away from the narrow way.

And some, not so flamboyant, would move among the flock paying lip service to the Lord but refusing to follow His commands except at their own pleasure. Peter and Paul would meet their share of these costumed souls—men who in the first century would call themselves Christians and continue to make a few expedient sacrifices to idols. Every age has its own souls with as much integrity as a dressed-up wolf, giving scandal to those outside the fold, slowing up the movement of the sheep, confusing them till they stray from the path.

Christianity is not a coat to be put over a man's naked nature. It is a new nature, transforming the whole man. And when faith is only skin deep it will betray itself in action.

"Beware of false spokesmen," He had said. And He had given the world the one infallible test of their truth.

It is the man who does the will of God, who produces the fruit of justice and mercy and love and sacrifice, who will enter the kingdom. If a man lives as God commands, with his feet on earth but his soul set on heaven, you shall know that his words are true.

And there on the mountain stood the absolute expression of truth, the One Who was the Word of God incarnate. His life was of one piece. In the end He would say: "In all things I have pleased the Father. I have done always the will of God, in all things."

As the Lamb of God He would offer His life for the salvation of men. He lived—and died—in love and sacrifice.

"*By their fruits you shall know them,*" He said. And no disguise will fit a wolf for the role of the Lamb. None but the true Vine can bring forth the fruit of holiness.

The sun rested on His brow like a crown. And men knew His voice was the voice of truth.

5

THE SAWDUST AND THE LOG*

H<small>E WAS</small> certainly no judge of character. They were right about that.

But in the beginning they did not understand why.

It was all very fine for Him to insist that He came to save sinners and not the good. But idealism could be carried too far. Some sinners do not want to be saved. Give a beggar money to feed his children and he will spend it on wine again. Give a thief a second chance and he'll pick your purse while you talk to him. . . .

It was, the Twelve knew, a waste of time to be nice to good-for-nothings. You had to look at the world realistically or be taken for a fool.

They did not like to see Him made ridiculous. But to their despair Jesus could not be made to see as they saw.

He could read men's hearts, name the sins of their past, with a glance. He had proven that. But still He treated every-one, even the scum of the streets, with the gravest courtesy. His scorn lashed only those who, like the Pharisees, pre-tended to be better than others. The riffraff, the red-nosed, shifty-eyed, sin-raddled people of the market place He greeted with almost courtly kindness.

The Twelve privately were of the opinion that Jesus was

* Matthew 7:1–5; Luke 6:41–45.

fortunate to have practical men such as they to protect Him. Holy men were famous for being a bit out of touch with the world, dreamers without prudence or judgment. And Jesus' own goodness, they felt, blinded Him to the faults of others.

They resolved to flank Him like a bodyguard, discreetly using their own judgment as they marshaled the mobs that wanted to see and touch their Master.

But after that day on the mountain by Capharnaum they were not so sure of themselves. For there, tucked into the vast tapestry of that sermon, was an unforgettable parable, the tiny tale of the sawdust and the log.

He had that morning given the world the first verbal profile of a Christian, a startling silhouette of white against black. Stroke by stroke he etched the bold portrait of a soul absolutely divorced from evil, in thought and hidden desire as well as in open action.

To follow Christ a man must be ready to cut off his own hand rather than commit sin. He must pray as other men love, offering all of himself without thought of reward or applause. He must be dedicated in complete integrity to the service of God.

And as Jesus spoke even the shyest soul felt the astonishing awareness that, though the task was tremendous, with God's help any man could indeed become perfect.

Perfection was an invigorating thought, fascinating as the far-off sound of any army, or the golden sky line of Jerusalem in the dawn. Listening to Him, a man could feel himself in the future, striding in humble majesty through a world too gross and pleasure-ridden to see the true glory of love and sacrifice. . . .

The Twelve, listening with the others on that mountain, pictured themselves as Jesus would want them to be, as surely they would be, paragons of virtue, shining lights of holiness.

And almost unaware they began thinking also of other people they knew, ticking off on their fingers the ones who could not possibly succeed in this new challenge.

After all, a man needed a certain greatness of nature, a response to the finer things, to understand what Jesus meant. Not everyone had that sensitivity. Hadn't Jesus said more than once that not everyone would be saved? That many are called but few are chosen? It was easy to see why!

The chosen cupped chins on hands and turned happy faces on their Master.

Then suddenly Peter clapped a hand to his left eye. Tears welled under his reddened lid, stinging and smarting. He rubbed it, muttering under his breath. Of all times to get something in your eye! That was the trouble with outdoor sermons. In a rabbi's study the wind didn't tousle your hair or invade your dignity with a bit of dust. He longed to pull down the lid and get the speck out, but this hardly seemed the place for a minor operation. Furtively, he blinked, trying to move the speck.

He stole a glance at the men nearest him. They were sitting extraordinarily still. Color burned in their cheeks. And no one spoke. Peter realized he had missed something important.

Jesus was staring directly at His Twelve, as if scanning the secrets of their souls.

"Judge not!" He said. And His gaze lay on them like a restraining hand on their smug preening of their own worthiness.

"Judge not, that you may not be judged. For with what judgment you judge, you shall be judged!"

He studied them solemnly, while the mountain wind chased cloud shadows over the grass-grown rock. And then He said:

"Why is it that you see the speck of sawdust that is in your brother's eye—and do not see the log that is in your own eye?"

It was a carpenter speaking—a workman who knew the nuisance of flying dust from a sawn timber, who knew, too, the joking exaggeration of men's talk that transformed a splinter of wood into a beam or a rafter.

"Or how is it," He said, "that you say to your brother: 'Let me get that bit of sawdust out of your eye'—and look!—a log is in your own eye?"

A chuckle broke through the soft whisper of the wind, the laughter of men who could picture from His voice the officious fussbudget who was bound to clean his friend's eye. Jesus, with His acute reportorial ear, had caught all the heavy-breathing chatter of busybodies everywhere, in carpenter's shops or beauty shops, in politics or in religion. . . .

"You hypocrite," said Jesus, "first take the beam out of your own eye, and then you shall be able to see to take the speck out of your brother's eye."

Two years later He would stand in the shadow of the Temple in Jerusalem to say to those who were ready to lynch a woman caught in adultery: "Let him who is without sin among you cast the first stone."

But He had spoken it first in the Sermon on the Mount— the humbling truth that no man could judge another's soul unless his own were clean.

"Can the blind lead the blind?" He had asked.

And Peter, his eye bloodshot and bleary, let his great head with its stiff gray beard sink on his chest. The speck of sawdust is nothing, thought Peter, an annoyance that could happen to anyone. And it is only kindness to help remove it. But who would want to have a man with a splinter inflaming his own eye prying yours open to swab out a speck?

Judge not, lest you be judged! The words pounded like a

storm wind in Peter's ears. And there under the Master's eye he saw suddenly the strange old truth that people see in others only what they know of themselves. The faults we recognize most quickly in our neighbors, the ones that offend us most, are those we have imbedded in our own souls.

The liar trusts no man's word. The gossip suspects all other tongues of malice. A man blinded by pride and by his own secret sins is in a great hurry to judge others, hoping to justify himself. But the good man?

Peter lifted his sun-wrinkled face and peered at Jesus.

There was the One Who was without sin—and He did not condemn. He did not condemn because He saw the good in all who came before Him. And He understood how to treat the part that was not yet clean.

Even now He smiled in understanding at Peter, and in a rush of gratitude the big fisherman felt tears of humility start in his eyes. In his heart he asked for that gift of love that would help him see as Christ sees—to find in others the reflection of God from his own soul.

The tears carried the speck out of Peter's eye. He fumbled, wiped his cheeks, and snorted as if to declare that he had a touch of a cold.

How would the world judge Jesus? As a blasphemer, a madman with delusions of grandeur, a criminal against the state. And there would be many who would find it amusing that the Man Who claimed to be the Son of the all-knowing God should have let His own betrayer nestle in the ranks of His disciples. He was naïve, they would say. No judge of character at all.

They would not begin to understand that as a Man even Christ did not judge. The day of judgment had not come. He would look at His enemies, clear-eyed, and ask His Father to forgive them.

And when in the years to come the course of duty would force some Christians by their offices to exercise judgment over others, they would do so in trembling humility, and in mercy, praying God to cleanse their own hearts first.

And till the end of time dust and cinders, motes and specks, would swirl in the wind to land in men's eyes, reminders of the Carpenter's tale.

6

THE HOUSE BUILT ON ROCK*

His voice carried on the mountain, mastering the wind. It traveled past the newly chosen Twelve at His feet to the hundreds listening on the slope. And that voice struck with an authority that would not be denied. No other man ever spoke that way.

It was as if He needed no other force but His own behind His commands and teaching. He spoke and there came from Him a sense of eternal power.

And those who heard Him were rapt, so welded to Him that the whole afternoon seemed lifted out of time.

They had come, this crowd, from the town of Capharnaum and beyond—from Galilee, from the Ten Cities of Decapolis, from Jerusalem and Judea, from the far province of Perea. They had heard of Him, of His miracles and teaching, and singly and by families they had come on foot and on donkey to Capharnaum where He was staying in the house of Peter.

What had brought them? Partly curiosity, the impulse to gawp and goggle at a celebrity and a good show. But even more it was the silent hope of the soul, the yearning reaching hope to find God's truth and love. God never made a soul without planting in it the certainty that it was made for more

* Matthew 7:24–29; Luke 6:48–49.

than death. And the soul will not rest till it finds life in Him.

So they came, some in holiday mood, exhilarated by travel and adventure, some querulous and half embarrassed, loudly announcing that they were not really taken in by miracles.

And Jesus, seeing them clogging the streets of Capharnaum, clamoring for Him to heal their sick and preach to them, left the town and led them out to the hills. A good brisk half hour's walk it is to the tiny mountain, longer and harder for the crowds to trek with their lunches and their babies, with children getting lost and men grumbling and women feeling the heat.

Then, when finally they settled among the grass and rocks, quieting slowly like a flock of monstrous migratory birds, He had begun to speak.

He spoke for more than two hours. And no one moved. No one grew restless. No one measured the sun as it moved down over the Galilean lake.

Later they would marvel at it themselves. But during those hours it seemed the most natural thing to sit and listen. They had not tired. His words were like the gift of life itself, lifting them into a new current, feeding and watering their inner beings.

Today the phrases of that Sermon on the Mount still flare like the first evening stars over the sea. The Lord's Prayer. The Beatitudes. The Golden Rule. Echoes from that sermon ring like distant trumpets: "Turn the other cheek. . . . Love your enemies. . . . Be you perfect. . . . No man can serve two masters. . . . Consider the lilies of the field. . . . Sufficient for the day is its own evil. . . . Judge not, lest you be judged. . . . Ask, and it shall be given you; seek, and you shall find. . . ."

It was an anthem of love—of God's love for man, and of the

love man must bear his God. It was the manifesto of Christianity, flung with humble majesty into the hearts of men.

They felt that love, those men and women on the slope. It fell like an embrace on all the pent-up loneliness of their souls, more precious than breath or light.

But more than love, they felt the power of those words.

This was no ordinary prophet. This was not simply an inspired man, eloquent, magnetic. This was *the* Man. Others spoke with authority but always it seemed a borrowed power. They quoted and covered themselves with the mantle of learning and postured and posed. They impressed people with what they had learned.

But this Jesus stood alone. And when He spoke men found themselves remembering that in Scripture God spoke—and there was Creation. Years later, John, one of the Twelve now at His feet, was to call Jesus the Word of God.

And as He spoke on that mountain the people knew that truth, not in words of theology or philosophy but in the quiet of their souls. As you can tell the difference between an inlet and the sea, between candle flame and the sun, so the men and women on the mountain recognized the power of this Jesus.

They were, as Matthew tells us, "full of admiration for His teaching. For He was teaching them as one having power, and not as the Scribes and Pharisees."

There are two kinds of ordinary teachers and spellbinders. One is anxious to have you understand that he is the known expert on a certain subject, and he practically bludgeons you into taking his words as golden. The other, having dazzled you, finds it more attractive to pretend to be nothing at all. Both are human.

But Jesus was neither pompous nor apologetic. He knew Himself for what and Who He was. And He wanted to be certain that no one should misunderstand or think that He considered Himself anything less than He was.

The immediate spell of that afternoon would fade. Centuries later men who were not there to hear would debate the full significance of His preaching. Was He a genius, one of many in different times and lands? Did His followers take Him more seriously than they should when they called Him divine?

He answered that question Himself when, at the very end of the Sermon on the Mount, He told the parable of the house built on rock.

"Everyone who hears My words," He said, "and *does* them, shall be like a wise man who built his house upon a rock."

His hands, spread slightly, pointing downward, seemed to evoke the mountain rock itself, the immovable eternal foundation of the earth.

"And the rain fell," He said, "and the floods came, and the winds blew. And they beat upon that house. And it did not fall, because it was founded on a rock!"

He bent His head slightly, till the evening dusk hid His eyes in shadow.

"And everyone who hears these My words," said Jesus, "and does them *not*, shall be like a foolish man who built his house on the sand."

Then, as He raised His glance again, a sadness close to anguish showed in His eyes.

"And the rain fell, and the floods came, and the winds blew. And they beat upon that house. And great was the fall thereof."

He who hears My words and does them—He had laid the challenge clear. *Live by what I say or be lost.*

An old proverb from Scripture, one of Solomon's words of

wisdom, echoed in the minds of those on the mountain. Again and again they had heard it, studied it in the synagogue.

"As a tempest that passes, so shall the wicked be no more. But the just are as an everlasting foundation. . . ."

If a man prayed the Our Father, the prayer He had taught them here, and lived by the truths of that prayer, if he would follow all the words of Christ as given to His apostles, then he would stand firm through all the furies of the storm. If he imbedded himself in Christ, nothing could harm his soul.

It is not, thought James, who was His kinsman, easy to dig a foundation on rock. Far easier to put up a shack by the shore such as fishermen use, or a little adobe hut on the ground. And many men who know better will still gamble on a poorly laid foundation, betting on fair weather for the future. We're a lazy bunch at heart, thought James, agreeing with all kinds of advice and doing nothing about it.

Some thirty years later, just before he was martyred, James would write a letter from Jerusalem to all Christians everywhere. And He would plead then: "Be you doers of the word, and not hearers only, deceiving yourselves!"

It can be backbreaking work, hewing a foundation for our spiritual home from the bedrock of virtue, of humility, of perseverance, and of love in Christ. The building of the home is done quickly. The laying of the foundation is what takes time.

There are no short cuts. We cannot simply listen admiringly and then hope to skim by without labor. True, no one can see what lies underground. The facade and landscaping of the house may impress men. We may fool even ourselves that we are living by the Word.

But the storm will come. The wind of temptation, the rain of fear and sorrow, the floods of pain and loneliness will beat on our souls, testing our capacity for stress and strain, blasting our weakness.

And if we have not built on the power of Christ, obedient to His rules, if we have not taken His word as the word of God, then the soul will shudder and groan and slide into the sea and the tempest, to be lost from sight.

The salvation of a soul is not a haphazard do-it-yourself business. It is the work of a man with God, and it must be done in God's own way.

The Word of God has the power to withstand any onslaught. And if we build with Him we shall stand till eternity.

7

PATCHES AND WINESKINS *

H E DID not behave the way people thought a holy man should. To put it bluntly, He was not dreary enough.

Everyone knew, or thought they did, that you could not be holy without being miserable. The Pharisees, who were supposed to be walking examples of how to please God, never enjoyed themselves in public. They displayed their righteousness by doing penance and fasting where everyone could see and hear them.

As for the prophets, every one of them from Elias to John the Baptist had cried out for men to weep for their sins and fast and to do penance.

That was the pattern of holiness as it had settled on Israel in those days. And Jesus of Nazareth did not seem to fit it at all.

True, He had once spent forty days fasting in the desert. But since then He had lived among the people, in the towns, as no prophet had ever done. He seemed now to pay scant attention to penance.

And He did not seem to object at all to having a good time. Even in His most serious moments a tide of quiet rejoicing surged from Him. As you stood near Him you remembered

* Matthew 9:16–17; Mark 2:21–22; Luke 5:33–39.

not Elias and the ravens but David dancing in joy before the ark of the covenant. . . .

As far as the Pharisees could see, for a man who evidently expected to set himself up as a religious leader Jesus' behavior was either idiocy or supreme cleverness. Jesus fit no known pattern. He was something entirely new.

They could not ignore Him. As Pharisees it was their duty to decide what should be thought and done about any religious problem. And Jesus presented a problem. In the public interest they sent teams of observers from Jerusalem.

They came to Capharnaum to ferret out the truth about Jesus. He handed it to them openly in one single day—what amounted in their eyes to a package of imprudence, scandal, and blasphemy.

He had been that afternoon in a private home besieged by crowds come to hear Him teach. The Pharisees edged close to Him to watch and listen. Suddenly overhead the roof opened up. Tiles were removed. And through the hole men lowered a stretcher directly in front of His nose—a wobbling contraption bearing the trembling body of a cripple. Jesus had looked at the cripple and said quietly:

"Your sins are forgiven you."

The Pharisees' thoughts gabbled in horror. Only God can forgive sins. . . .

Jesus knew their thoughts. To them He said, "Which is easier to say: 'Your sins are forgiven,' or, 'Arise and walk'? But, so you will know that the Son of Man has power on earth to forgive sins——"

Before their eyes He had cured that cripple.

And right after that Jesus had gone out to the lakeside and chosen a new disciple. He had picked a publican—the tax collector named Matthew.

The Pharisees sucked their teeth in fresh shock. Publicans

(tax collectors) were considered unclean and sinful men, polluted by association with the Roman occupation forces, fattening on graft and thievery. What kind of holy man chooses such a disciple?

Jesus said to Matthew: "Follow Me."

And Matthew was so deliriously excited at being chosen by Jesus that he insisted on throwing a great party to celebrate. He had a fine home, many friends—mostly publicans like himself. He invited them, and they came. So did Jesus and the other four disciples—Peter and Andrew, James and John.

It was incredible that Jesus should risk His reputation by going to Matthew's party. To call an obvious sinner to a new life as a disciple was one thing. To feast with him on food that might even have been earned by graft, in the company of ritually unclean sinners, was another.

Most of Capharnaum trooped along to watch the festivities. Tables were spread in the torchlit garden, with cushions on the grass for guests to recline on. The odor of roast meat mingled in the air with laughter and song. And in the road people craned their necks in curiosity and good will and vicarious pleasure.

The Pharisees and their Scribes were there, ready to destroy Jesus once and for all. It was plainly their duty to rescue the poor innocent common folk around them from His spell. He had given them the perfect opening. They were ready to pounce on it.

From strategic spots in the throng they began their campaign, calling out to the four disciples who sat feasting in the garden.

"Look at your Master! He eats with sinners and publicans!"

"This is a new kind of holy man—working miracles one minute and carousing the next!"

"If your Master is so good, why does He defile himself by dining with sinners? Tell us that!"

Jesus heard their taunts. And He Himself answered in a voice carrying clearly across the low vine-grown fence.

"It is not the healthy who need a physician," He called, "but the sick! I have not come to call the just, but sinners— to repentance!"

Repentance? What did this Man, reclining cozily at table, know of *repentance?*

The way of repentance lay in fasting, suffering, and weeping for one's sins. Prophets never feasted. Did Elias ever go to a party? Or John the Baptist?

The Pharisees beckoned the four disciples out to the road. Faces pressed nearer in the orange glow to watch.

One Pharisee pointed to some gaunt-faced solemn men on the fringes of the crowd. "Look—there are some of John the Baptist's disciples. *They* fast. *They* pray often. And we Pharisees fast and pray. Then why is it that you go around eating and drinking and making merry?

"Is that the way to be holy? Is that what your Master teaches? No fasting? No penance?"

Before the disciples could speak, Jesus was beside them, a smile gleaming on His lean young face, meeting the attack with a question of His own.

"Can you make the friends of the bridegroom fast—while the bridegroom is still with them?" asked Jesus.

Questions froze on the Pharisees' pursed lips. *The bridegroom*—echoes of Scripture eddied around the phrase. In prophecy God spoke of His love for His people as the love of bridegroom for bride. . . . Could this Jesus dare call Himself the Bridegroom?

In the darkness the Baptist's disciples caught their breath. When, a moment before, the Pharisees had pointed to them, they had been taken by surprise, embarrassed to be used as a weapon against Him. Now His words drew them. Only a few weeks before they had asked John about Jesus. And John had called Him—the Bridegroom!

Gravely, earnestly, Jesus continued: "The days will come when the Bridegroom shall be taken away from them. Then they shall fast in those days."

He paused for an instant, His eyes commanding attention. And, there outside Matthew's gate, He told a parable that held the tremendous truth about Himself—a tiny tale of patches and wineskins.

"No one," said Jesus, "takes a piece from a new garment to patch an old one. If he does, he has not only torn and ruined the new one, but also the piece from the new one will not agree with the old!"

A woman perched on a step grunted. The patch wouldn't match—or hold! You can't piece soft threadbare cloth with firm new stuff. She cocked her head thoughtfully.

"And no man," He said, "puts new wine into old wineskins. Otherwise the new wine will break the wineskins, and it will be spilled, and the wineskins will be ruined as well."

He grinned in the torchlight and spread His hands in a half shrug.

"New wine must be put into new wineskins. Then—both are preserved!"

Who there had not heard and smelled the strange explosion that came when a man did try foolishly to put new vintage into last year's sheep or goatskin container? Wine, fermenting and expanding, burst the skin, splattering to the ground. The wine was, you might say, alive. The old skin, stretched and dry and worn, was lifeless. It could not begin to hold the fresh wine.

But what had patches and wineskins to do with fasting or with the "Bridegroom"?

Years later men would understand that He spoke then of the Old Testament and the New, and of the sharp break between them. They would see that in Jesus the whole world was made new, and that to receive His truth men must also be born again in newness.

The old garment had been good but it was outworn. You could not patch it with the new. The new wine of Christianity could not be compressed in the rigid skin of the past without bursting its bonds. . . .

Not till after the ascension, not till the Bridegroom was gone from them, would men see that meaning in the parable. But as He stood before them that night—the One Who broke the patterns, the One all-new—they caught in their hearts another part of the truth of that parable.

As the song and laughter of the feast drifted out to them, these men and women knew that in Jesus they had met a new kind of Master—the One in Whom holiness was a living cause of joy. The crowd stirred. The thought of joyful holiness was new wine indeed. . . .

The days were coming when the followers of Jesus would fast and do penance. He had not come to deny the value of mortification and penance. He did come to show men a new spirit toward God. Even in suffering a Christian must know joy in his soul, in sure awareness of union with Him.

The time of the prophets and the Pharisees was over. The time of Christ was beginning. And those who heard Him that night sensed without knowing why that these days when He was with them were precious, a festival to be treasured.

Jesus, raising His hand in farewell salute, turned back to Matthew and his celebration.

The Pharisees stood silently watching Him go. The light

from a torch flickered on their faces. And to some in the crowd it seemed that their cheeks, set in open disapproval of Jesus, had the pale stretched leathery look of last year's wineskins.

8

THE COCKLE IN THE FIELD*

H E W A S, men agreed, a most unusual preacher.

He stood in the bow of the old ship pulled up on the sand, the wind playing in His long brown hair. His cheeks seemed hardy and weather-beaten as the boat timbers themselves. He stood with dignity, as if this were the most natural place in the world to teach about heaven, here on the beach where men mended nets, where skins of drinking water hung on rope trestles and the smell of fish was everywhere. His voice carried buoyantly over the ruffling edgewaters, over the sough of grasses and the grumble of the sand under the feet of children.

Palestine was no stranger to street preachers. Every year a new group rose like a gaggle of geese. Some shouted with glittering eyes. Some screamed for revolution. Others, pale-lipped and droop-eyed, quoted Scripture in endless whispers. And none lasted long.

But this one was different. He spoke with authority. He did not rant. And He was a man's man, taller than most, strong-armed and healthy, contemptuous of platitudes.

The people of Capharnaum came to listen to Him out of curiosity. They knew Peter, Andrew, James, and John. They

* Matthew 13:24–30, 36–43.

wanted to hear the Master the fishermen followed. They stayed not out of curiosity but out of love and wonder.

He spoke to them of the kingdom of heaven. And He spoke in parables, in tales rooted in everyday life yet rising as if to flower in God.

One thing about this Jesus, they said, He did not shy away from difficult problems. He was a superb realist. He did not go around spitting at the whole worldful of people the way some preachers did. Nor did He see things through a misty dream of happiness. He saw life as it was, full of good and evil.

He leaned now from the bow, His eyes scanning the crowd yet seeming at the same time to focus on each soul separately. And He answered a question He saw yet unspoken in His listeners, a question that has bedeviled men since the beginning of time.

Why does the good God let evil flourish in His world?

Why is it that the wicked seem able to live their days undisturbed, crowding out the good, flaunting themselves in the face of heaven? Is God too weak to assert Himself? Or is it really wiser to live as one pleases, instead of as God pleases?

There were in that crowd men who suffered oppression from the Roman conquerors, men who had to bow and scrape when Herod, that monster-pervert king, passed down the road. Facing Jesus that day by the shore were men who had been cheated by their employers, men bled to poverty by usurers, women whose lives had been ruined by unpunished evil, or whose children had died because of someone's callousness.

It was an ordinary group of decent God-fearing folk that gathered on that shore, and they faced as we do today the puzzle of good and evil.

And Jesus said to them:

"The kingdom of heaven is like a man who sowed good seed in his field."

They stirred a little, remembering the parable He had already told them of the good seed that fell on the wayside and among thorns. But this was a different story, a new glimpse into the mysterious ways of God.

Jesus continued: "But while men were asleep his enemy came and oversowed cockle among the wheat and went his way."

Cockle? You didn't have to be a farmer to know what cockle was. Though the weed is rare here it is more common than dandelions in Palestine. It is actually what our botanists today call *Lolium temulentum,* and in some places it is called darnel.

Cockle has two unusual characteristics. For one thing, if it is eaten it produces a strange drunken dizziness in beasts and in men. Cattle that nibble it lurch around the pasture. For another, like so many weeds, cockle is a clever deceiver. It looks very much like grain when it is young, only its ear is slenderer than an ear of rye.

But whoever heard of growing cockle on purpose? The people on the shore grinned at each other. It was a funny thought, but still rather devilishly clever!

"And when the good blades of grain had sprung up," said Jesus, "and begun to form their ears, then the cockle appeared also. And the servants of the farmer came to him and said: 'Sir, did you not sow good seed in the field? Then where did this cockle come from?'

"And he said to them: 'An enemy has done this.'

"And the servants asked: 'Do you want us to go and weed the cockle out?'

"But he said: 'No—lest perhaps while you go pulling out the cockle you uproot the grain with it. Let them both grow until the harvest, and in the time of the harvest I will say to my reapers: Gather first the cockle and bind it into bundles to burn. But gather the wheat into the barn.'"

What did it mean? To some on the shore that day the message was clear, as fresh and real as the bread in their hands. To others it was still a mystery. But we have Jesus' own explanation, as He gave it that night to His disciples after supper in Peter's house.

They had learned by now that He often deliberately cloaked His preaching in parables because it was not yet time for Him to declare Himself to the world as the Son of God. But the disciples knew too from experience that He would explain the parables to them, and that explanation would be preserved through the ages so that all men might hear and understand.

"Tell us," they said, "the meaning of the parable of the cockle."

In the light of the brazier coals His face seemed suddenly ageless. Where a moment before there had been the gentle humor of mealtime banter, there was now solemnity bordering on majesty. And His voice, though low, framed each word with infinite care.

"He that sowed the good seed is the Son of Man," said Jesus. "And the field is the world.

"And the good seed are the children of the kingdom. But the cockle are the children of the wicked one. And the enemy that sowed them is—the devil.

"But the harvest is the end of the world. And the reapers are the angels."

A coal in the brazier flared a sudden orange, quivered, and fell to the grate below. The slight sound of it seemed thunderous in that silent room. And Jesus' voice continued, even lower than before:

"Just as cockle is gathered up and burnt in the fire, so shall it be at the end of the world.

"The Son of Man shall send His angels and they shall gather out of His kingdom all scandals, and all those who work iniquity. And they shall cast them into the furnace of fire. There shall be weeping and gnashing of teeth."

He raised His head, and His voice rose again from sadness.

"And then shall the just shine like the sun in the kingdom of their Father. He that has ears to hear—let him hear."

He stood up and went to the doorway, looking out into the moonlit night. The Twelve did not move, each wrapped in his own study of the teaching they had heard.

At the end of the world the wicked would be punished—that they had always known. But from the Lord Himself they knew now that God had no intention of weeding out evil until the end. So long as men lived the wicked would thrive and nothing would be done about it.

". . . *lest you uproot the good grain with it. . . .*"

Simon, the one they called the Zealot, spread his fingers upward in the light. He was not a farmer. But as a child he had worked his mother's vegetable garden in the back yard. And he still remembered the day he had tried to weed it when the seedlings were small. He had destroyed a whole planting of lettuce in his zeal to pull out the weeds! Weed roots are strong and deep, he remembered, and as you pull them out whole clods and lumps of earth come with them, ripping up good seed at the same time.

It was, thought Simon, a greater kindness to the good, really, for the Lord to let the wicked live undisturbed.

Andrew sighed beside him. Once, he thought, the great God had unleashed a flood to destroy the wicked and it took almost a miracle to save Noah and his family. Once He had destroyed the sinfulness of Sodom and Gomorrah, and had to send angels to rescue Lot and his family. Even God cannot take time out to protect every one of the good while He strikes the wicked down in their tracks!

And, thought Peter, the cockle and the grain look a good deal alike. True, grain grows taller than the cockle by far. But might not a slow-growing ear of grain be mistaken for a weed? Or a slow-growing soul be struck down by the reapers before it proved itself?

He was suddenly most grateful to the Lord of the harvest for his prudent patience!

There is none of us, he thought, whose roots are not entwined with the roots of others, as the good grain is with the cockle. Even inside ourselves evil roots along with grace. Peter stared at the fire in his own hearth and shivered, a prayer in his heart.

And Jesus stood alone staring out at the sleeping town where, as everywhere, there were children of the kingdom side by side with children of the enemy.

He would sow the seed of truth in the souls of many. His servants would tend the harvest through the years—these disciples and those of the centuries to come. Again and again His servants would cry out to the Lord to know why the good field of the world was overridden with the weeds of sin. They would fret, their hands itching to destroy the work of the devil.

But until the harvest the grain and the cockle would grow together. Such is the way of the Lord.

9

THE NET*

THE WIND off the lake shore, drifting down from the cold mountains to the valley heat, stirred warning waves as it sped toward the town of Capharnaum. Date palms bowed lightly and whispered. Fishermen spat on their fingers and held them knowingly to the breeze. There would be no fishing this night if this mood of the wind held.

Lying low, cupped beneath the level of the world's oceans, this lake could stir to violence as steep as any true sea, more sudden than summer thunder. The men of Galilee called this water Kinnereth, which meant harp-shaped, and in its calmer moments there were some who thought the waves did make music under the sunlit air. The fishermen were not inclined to such poesy.

The lake was the focus of Capharnaum's life. True, the town had become a caravan resting place, a bustling, rustling bazaar where a man could hear almost as many tongues as in Jerusalem. But it was to the fishing boats and their men that the town owed its fame. The catch of Capharnaum traveled fresh, dried, or brined to every corner of Palestine.

Jesus stood now, framed by the graying waters, gusts tugging at His long dark hair, His white tunic tossed by the

* Matthew 13:47–51.

breeze, talking to the fishermen and their families. On the tiny slopes above clustered an audience drawn from the market place, buyers and sellers and gawkers and peasants, all a bit out of place on the lake front.

But He seemed at home. And Capharnaum fishermen had given up wondering at His way of dealing with their lake. They remembered—who could forget?—the day He had come striding down the shore to call His disciples. Peter and his brother Andrew had been standing on that promontory where the grass grows tall, testing a net in the water. And He had called to them:

"Come, follow Me—and I will make you fishers of men."

And they followed Him. And a bit farther down the shore He had come to James and John. They had been sitting in their father's boat. Their father, old Zebedee, had worked with them, mending a net quite calmly. And Jesus had called those two sons, and they had followed Him.

Fishers of men—it was a phrase the men turned over in their minds as they rode the waves in their boats, a phrase to puzzle anyone coming from the mouth of a Carpenter!

But no other carpenter was ever so at ease with water. This Jesus could silence an angry storm with one word. He could walk the waves as if they were meadow-green turf. Even Peter, that hulking giant, had been seen to walk dry over the tossing water with Jesus till he grew afraid and fell in!

This Carpenter had a fisherman's eye for weather. And an uncanny knack of reading the minds of the fish, you might say. Toss your net where He pointed, and you had a catch to dazzle the market place.

The fishermen of Capharnaum were willing to accept Him and listen to Him as if He were one of them.

He had been preaching on the water front for a week now, casting His thought in the tales called parables, picturing for

His listeners the kingdom of heaven. And until now He had dressed these parables in the costume of the farm and field, of the bazaar and the home, in the everyday life of the men and women munching and listening above under the palms.

Now, with a smile and one outstretched hand as if both to display and to embrace the fishing fleet, Jesus said: ·

"The kingdom of heaven is like a net cast into the sea. . . ."

The crowd on the slope stared suddenly at the long drying drapes of net as if they had actually never seen a net before. The fishermen looked wise and shifted their weight from one hip to another, eyes bent intently on the shell and stone under their toes.

The nets of Capharnaum were formidable, stretching as long as a quarter of a mile, but narrow—only some nine or ten feet wide. Hand-knotted, meticulously mended and groomed, these nets literally cupped and sieved the water, sweeping all loitering fish before them. Weighted with lead on one border, sustained by giant cork floats on the other, they required a band of men to manipulate them.

Half the men would stand on the shore, net folded in front of them. The other half went out in the boat, carrying the end of the net with them while the boat sailed a wide arc of water to a point farther down on the shore. Shore and net then made a long pointed oval, a trap slowly drawn tight at both ends, gathered in, pulled into an ever smaller arc till the day's harvest lay loosely bundled on the beach.

Some fishermen did venture out farther into the lake, casting at times in the bluer water where the bottom lay twenty fathoms deep. But for the most part the teeming waters yielded their catch more easily in the dappled shallows, where sudden mountain-bred storms did not threaten the life of a boat.

"The kingdom of heaven is like a net cast into the sea," He

said, "gathering fish of every kind. And when it was filled the
men drew it out and, sitting by the shore, they chose and
gathered the good fish into containers, and the bad they
threw away."

Up on the palm-shaded hill the people nodded, remembering that they had come to take for granted the sight of
fishermen sorting the net's haul in great flipping shining shim-
mering piles of fish. Certainly, thought the bazaar merchants,
the smell of that work traveled with these men wherever they
went. But who would quibble over an odor? The fish they
did bring to market were perfect.

The fishermen eyed Jesus solemnly and grunted. These
waters boasted at least twenty-two kinds of fish—some said
thirty. Most were edible, except those which were scaleless,
like the special Galilean catfish. Scripture, God's own Law,
forbade the eating of any fish without scales. The catfish had
to be removed, and any stray shellfish, undersize fish, muti-
lated fish, and the scrapings of the lake bottom. Sorting took
hours of a man's day, a practiced eye, skilled hands. It was,
some said, a shame a man couldn't invent a selective net. But
to get the best in fish, you had to drag up everything at once
and do the selection later. Fishermen knew that, and in
the way of practical men they had small patience with day-
dreamers. . . .

But what had a net of fish to do with the kingdom of
heaven? Was He saying men were no more than fish to be
dragged wholesale to shore? It was not, thought one friend
of Zebedee, too complimentary a picture. He raised a scarred
face in challenge.

But Jesus continued:

"So will it be at the end of the world. The angels shall go
out and separate the wicked from among the just. And they

shall cast them into the furnace of fire, and there shall be weeping and the gnashing of teeth."

In the wind-tossed silence as He finished, the men of Capharnaum pondered that parable.

Like the cockle and the wheat it was, thought Andrew, this tale of the net. Good men and bad were to be drawn into the kingdom of heaven. And they would not be separated until the final judgment. The net was not selective. It clasped within itself fine clean fish and slimy lake greens and mud and rock and monsters of the deep, making no distinction, sweeping all before it to the fisherman's mercy and justice.

Judgment would come, swift and certain, at the end of the world. Till then the kingdom of heaven would be a motley affair with saints and sinners, hypocrites and mystics side by side—a sight to annoy and scandalize many. It would not be orderly. It would not be a sweet-smelling, exclusive society such as the Pharisees enjoyed.

But as fishermen knew, there was no other way to be sure no good fish escaped!

Men would grow impatient, critical, disgusted at rubbing shoulders with others in this strange invisible divine net. They would wonder more than once why credentials weren't investigated, obvious renegades removed by some board of examiners, ousted before they injured others.

Peter, his cheeks reddening in the wind, frowned. I can judge fish, thought he. But who is to judge men caught in the net of God? The fish do not judge each other! And a broad grin spread like a wave over his beard, exploding into laughter. What kind of herring would it be to set itself up as arbiter of the moral qualifications of a catfish?

No man can judge another with finality. Even the Twelve,

whom He called to be the fishers of men, could not know each other's true worth.

Of those Twelve it might have seemed that Peter would not pass inspection. Did he not argue back to the Master more than once? Didn't Jesus Himself rebuke him? And James and John—didn't they squabble right up to the last days of Jesus' life over who was to have the best seat in heaven?

But Judas? No one gave him much thought, you know. A quiet one, diligent with the alms and small purchases of the Twelve, he seemed quite passable. Even at the Last Supper, who thought of Judas when Jesus spoke?

As the years passed men would remember the parable of the net and find curious comfort in the thought that not men but angels would judge, not now but at the end of time.

As Jesus left the shore to go back to Peter's house His smile embraced fishermen and merchants. And there were those who would say that He seemed to spread over all an unseen tender net of love, drawing all in His wake.

10

HIDDEN TREASURE AND A PEARL *

HE POSSESSED joy as if it were His birthright. And that was, in itself, a most unusual thing.

People watched Him closely, peering at Him from trees and over half-closed gates. They dogged His footsteps and crowded up to Him. And they could not quite understand Him.

He certainly was not what you might call happy-go-lucky. He had been seen to weep with pity. He had at times a look of unbearable sadness. He could argue and debate most seriously with the keenest minds, and win. He had been known to cope with taxes and with government agents. He was not an idiot, dancing along the road.

But He was, quite definitely, not a melancholy man. He could and did sing in a fine deep voice—the Psalms, mostly, but an old folk song or two as well. He rollicked with little children and enjoyed Himself at weddings. He could turn a joke. And His laugh, though rare, had echoed over the lake like a gust from heaven itself.

Other men had come, many times before, to talk to the world of God and heaven and good and evil, and most of them had been a sad-faced lot. Warnings of woe thundered

* Matthew 13:44–46.

from their lips, and they denied themselves all luxuries, even, it seemed, the simple indulgence of a smile. False prophets, droop-jawed, pale-cheeked, they had mourned and moaned and sniveled over the world, and been forgotten. No one had been able to listen to them for more than an hour.

But this Jesus was different.

He had not happiness, which is a passing thing, the flower of an hour's sunshine—nor delight, which is a thing of pleasure in mind or body. He had joy—as firm as the trunk of a tree, surging upward in a constant current, supporting Him as the sea buoys a boat. It was almost tangible, this certainty of joy. You could sense it in Him even when He turned in anger on the Pharisees, or stood in grief with a widow weeping for her only son.

It seemed to spring from the possession of a secret, an inner knowledge that bred a glory nothing could destroy. And it was the mysterious secret of that joy as much as anything that drew people to Him.

After all, He had nothing a man could see to rejoice about. He had nothing. His life, for the most part, was not exciting. He was not a spectacular success. Even His miracles made Him enemies. He was most unpopular in His home town of Nazareth. Some of His relatives—not the cousins who were among His disciples, but others—were openly jealous of Him.

The people of Capharnaum, especially the men of the harbor, had also wondered for a long time what it was that lured some of their own friends to follow Jesus. Peter and his brother Andrew, and Zebedee's sons James and John, were good conservative fellows with a reliable future in the fishing fleet. Yet they had thrown over everything—family, boats, money—to traipse after this Jesus.

And they did not seem to regret it at all.

Why? The question bothered people intensely. They listened to Him, they spied on Him, and still they wondered. When He preached, up in the hillside synagogue, or here by the waters of the lake, they found part of the answer. But always it escaped them.

He spoke of a kingdom, the kingdom of heaven. And yet He had not a gold piece to His name. He had not given these Twelve followers anything at all. They would have gone hungry often if it were not for the kindness of some of the families in town.

Some of the fishermen and some of the traders from the bazaar had thought Jesus meant to lead a revolution against the Roman occupation forces and free the kingdom of Israel. That would have been a secret to give anyone joy. But He did not seem to be plotting an armed uprising. He had even run away from a crowd that clamored for Him to be their king.

Then what was it?

This day He was sitting on the prow of Peter's old fishing boat, and the throng had come as usual to the water's edge, bringing lunches of dates and cheese and bread to eat while they listened.

And Jesus said to them:

"The kingdom of heaven is like a treasure hidden in a field. And a man, having found it, hid it, and in his joy at having found it he goes and sells all that he has and buys that field."

Hidden treasure! It was a dream quite possible of fulfillment in a land like Palestine where century after century wars and invasions had forced people to leave house and home and flee.

Even today a random spade occasionally turns up the valuables of thousands of years past. The Dead Sea Scrolls are only a small sample of what has been hidden and not yet found.

"And again," said Jesus, His eye measuring the Greek merchants from the Capharnaum bazaars and the foreigners from passing caravans idling on the shore, "the kingdom of heaven is like a merchant seeking pearls. When he found one pearl of great price he went and sold all that he had and bought it."

And Jesus raised His hands, cupped together as if catching a treasure in the sunlight and holding it.

A pearl of great price—and a buried treasure. Has there ever been a time when men's hearts have not been captured by such thoughts? Anyone would sacrifice to buy the field, if he knew gold were hidden in it. Who would not give up everything else to gain a pearl worth a fortune?

And yet a man might walk over the patch of ground and see nothing but weeds. Only an astute and careful trader could tell a good pearl from a bad one. One pearl could look as big and round and lustrous as another, and still be flawed and worthless.

The men on that shore looked at Jesus, and He knew their thoughts and He smiled and bent His head.

If a man only knew! There was the spearhead of the parable. If men recognized the infinite treasure of heaven when it was in their grasp, then they would go and sell all they had to gain it—"in joy at having found it."

The problem was in knowing and recognizing the treasure.

Some would come on it by chance, as if they were digging in the field and the spade clinked on the coins. Some would be prepared by training to find it, educated to detect its presence, like the pearl trader, whose fingers knew the smoothness of the perfect pearl.

By chance or by training—every soul in the world would have its moment of decision.

And, having found the treasure of heaven, they would be

like fools in the world's eyes—sacrificing everything for a round white ball the size of a pea or for a barren plot of ground. That is part of the price of any treasure—the time when you look like a fool.

Who are the treasure seekers of today? We do not have many pearl merchants. Even pirate treasure is in scarce supply. But we have our own. The uranium prospector, living in rags and misery, isolated from society, waiting in patience to make his strike. The scientist, sacrificing pleasure and rest to give the last ounce of strength and study to discover an equation that ninety per cent of the world will neither understand nor appreciate. The athlete, disciplining his body to conquer the Channel, to win an international championship, or to master a remote mountain. The woman denying herself comfort to put a son through college or further her husband's career.

Each one of those has sighted a goal that is a treasure in his own eyes.

And there are those whose treasure cannot be measured in the world's scale, neither in ambition nor wealth, in mental or physical triumph, not even in human love. There are today thousands of souls who have glimpsed the secret treasure of the kingdom of heaven and who are prepared to claim it at any cost.

And they look like fools to the world. No other treasure is as hidden from the casual eye as the treasure of union with God. The shining glory of gold may be hidden in an old rag. A pearl is concealed in the callused shell of the oyster. But the treasure of Christianity is hidden in a life of humility and of pain and of apparent death.

Yet the knowledge of that treasure was the secret of His joy—and the secret of the joy of all the souls who have followed Him through the centuries. It is the secret of the quiet ecstasy of housewives and of hermits, of martyrs and of businessmen—the exhilaration of the certain knowledge that heaven is by grace theirs.

There has never been a melancholy saint. A man who glooms and mourns over his religion has not found the pearl of great price. Even in stress and discipline, even in moments of desolation and pain, when all happiness and delight are gone, still there remains in the children of His kingdom an abiding joy. It can distress a man to sell all that he has. He may weep to part with what he holds dear. But the joy of the treasure he has found will sustain him through any ordeal.

That joy is yours and mine today. And we must not hide it. For more than anything it is proof that we have found the one thing worth having—the love of God. And our joy will draw others to share the same inexhaustible treasure.

Can we complain because of the price of the pearl?

11

THE DEBTOR WHO DID NOT FORGIVE *

H<small>E WALKED</small> by the shore as simply as a child, as if at any moment He might skip a flat stone across the low waves or pick a shell off the gravelly sand. He was, thought Peter, an enigma. His grip could make a strong man falter. The voice that now hummed a tune to the wind could shake like thunder when roused. His strength Peter understood and respected. It was His gentleness that disturbed him.

The blunt-faced, wide-footed fisherman tramped behind Him on the beach, wondering. Peter was not by nature a thinker. He was an outdoor man, a man of action. His mind was much like a good fishing boat, sturdy, hard-working, but slow. At times he seemed to lumber through the oceans of truth, but always he steered his course to the end.

And this day a question bothered Peter, a problem that had rumbled inside him for months. The question was about forgiveness.

Again and again Jesus, His long lean face aglow with love, had said that, to love God, you must forgive not only your friends but especially your enemies. You must, for the love of God, forgive quickly and completely.

* Matthew 18:23–35.

On that one unforgettable afternoon on the mountainside, when Jesus had first preached to the Twelve together, He had taught them to pray with the razor-edged plea:

"Forgive us our trespasses, as we forgive those who trespass against us."

Peter sighed. He knew from experience that forgiveness was not easy. His own temper was famous throughout this, his home town of Capharnaum. Everyone from his mother-in-law to his fellow fishermen had at times found it hard to forgive him.

And he did not forgive others easily, either. He had practiced valiantly at this art of forgiveness for the year or more that he had known Jesus. He was beginning to get the knack of it. But still, if the truth were known, it seemed to him an unmanly business, almost a sign of weakness.

One point especially bothered him. It did not seem either practical or just to go on forgiving the same man for the same thing again and again. Sometime there must be an end to patience, a time for vengeance, or, at the least, a time to put an end to the monotony of forgiveness. You could, felt Peter, stretch mercy too far and lose your dignity. There was a limit, wasn't there?

So Peter asked Jesus the question we all feel like asking once in a while:

"Lord, just how many times must I forgive a man? Seven times?"

Jesus turned with a smile of indescribable strength and dignity.

"Not seven times, Peter, but seventy times seven shall you forgive!"

They were down by the Sea of Galilee there in Capharnaum, in sight and smell of the drying nets and the sun-kissed waves. And Jesus settled Himself on the wall above the sand,

and the Twelve sat beside Him to listen as He told the parable of the debtor who did not forgive.

"The kingdom of heaven," He began, "is like a king who decided to take an audit of the affairs of his servants."

Matthew, who had some experience with finance, having been a tax collector until Jesus called him as a disciple, nodded knowingly. But the others, though they were poor men, knew enough of the ways of rulers to grasp the picture.

It was, they knew, common practice for the higher servants of a rich man to borrow his money for a few private investments of their own. To a point, this was an accepted practice. But of course sometimes a man could be carried away and stretch the tolerance of even the best of rulers!

"And when he began to go over the accounts," said Jesus, "a man was brought to him who owed him ten thousand talents."

Ten thousand talents! The silver coin called the talent equaled about six thousand Greek drachmas. Ten thousand talents was more than any man could hope to earn in ten lifetimes. In our money today it would come to about fifteen million dollars!

"And since he did not have the money to pay his debt," said Jesus, "his lord commanded that he should be sold, and his wife and children and all that he had, so that some payment could be made.

"But that servant, falling down before his lord, pleaded with him, saying: 'Have patience with me—and I will pay you all that I owe!'"

Matthew grinned in his short black beard. No one could ever make enough to pay such a debt, not with the taxes the way they were those days.

"And the lord of that servant," said Jesus earnestly, "being moved with pity, let him go and forgave him that debt."

He turned a bit, His eyes fixed on the streets of the town above them.

"But when that servant went out he found one of his fellow servants who owed him—a hundred pennies."

Matthew sniffed. A hundred Greek pennies was a nice figure, but next to ten thousand talents it was only a grain of dust.

"And he grabbed his fellow and throttled him, saying: 'Pay what you owe!'

"And his fellow servant, falling down, begged him, saying: 'Have patience with me, and I will pay you all!' "

Peter grinned. As Jesus spoke those words they were the perfect echo of the words the first servant had used pleading for his lord's mercy.

"But," said Jesus, "he would not, and he went and cast him in prison till he paid the debt.

"Now his fellow servants, seeing what was done, were very much grieved, and they went and told their lord all that was done.

"Then the lord called him and said to him: 'You wicked servant, I forgave you all the debt because you begged me for mercy! Should you then not have had compassion also on your fellow servant even as I had compassion on you?'

"And his lord, being angry, delivered him to the torturers until he paid all his debt."

Jesus stood then, His eyes seeming to sink in sudden sadness as He spoke in a voice low as the whisper of death.

"So also shall My Heavenly Father do to you, if you forgive not every one his brother from your heart."

Matthew sucked his upper lip. He saw clearly the difference between the debts. What man owes God, the debt the Lord cancels out of pity, is far greater than ten thousand talents or ten thousand thousand talents. And what a man may owe me, the outrage I may be asked to forgive, is a small matter by comparison—a few pennies' worth against the national debt.

But tears came to Peter's eyes. He had been setting himself up as a lord, and he was, after all, only a servant. The lord had the right and power to do as he pleased with a mere hireling—and he chose to use his power to forgive. But for one servant to refuse forgiveness then to another who was his equal was ridiculous.

And Peter remembered the days when he and his brother Andrew were little. How often he had seen a boy caught by his parents in mischief go and take out his shame by bullying another child. How often he had heard a hired fisherman come home after a day of mistakes and explode with anger at his wife's spilled soup. Even as a child Peter had known how small and unmanly such anger was.

And yet he had dared ask how often he should forgive! He dropped his face in his hands. What was there anyone could do to offend him that could compare with his own offenses against God?

"Forgive us our trespasses as we forgive those who trespass against us."

It was, thought Peter, a forthright proposition. Show mercy and you will have infinite mercy. Demand vengeance and you will receive the punishment you yourself deserve. That prayer is, thought Peter, an eminently practical way of dealing with hotheads like us.

And for the first time he realized that forgiveness took more than human strength. Not weakness but the power of the living God moved in mercy.

Shamefaced, he raised his head and met the deep eyes of his Lord. The thunder had left His glance. In its place was the fire of infinite love.

And He did not ask, as another might have done:

"How many times have I forgiven you, Peter? And how many more times must I do so?"

He had forgiven, and forgotten.

He leaped down to the sand, walking almost in flirtation with the waters lapping on the beach. As the Twelve rose to follow Him they saw in Him no trace of hurry. To look at Him, you would not think Him capable of anger.

But the echo of those words: "So shall My Father do to you," seemed caught in the endless waves of the Galilean Sea.

12

THE FRIEND AT MIDNIGHT *

He was completely manly—and utterly childlike. It was a combination to puzzle men for centuries, a contradiction understood only by those who are close to God.

No one could accuse Him of weakness. He had a carpenter's muscles, hardened by daily contact with timbers, ax, and saw. The self-discipline of an athlete firmed the lean litheness of His body. Once, it was known, He had fasted forty days, starved Himself in a grueling battle of body and spirit in the gaunt stretches of the desert to the south. And He could ride out a tempest in a small boat, so unafraid that He actually napped in the heaving prow.

He could and did parry the sophisticated heckling of the Pharisees, debate with the keenest minds in Palestine. He had faced mobs poised with murder in their eyes, the sharp stones of death clutched in their fists. He was every inch a man—mature, self-possessed, filled with dignity.

And yet He was guileless, swift to love, humble, joyous as a child.

More than once He had swept up a barefoot tangle-haired urchin from the crowd by a village well, holding the flushed cheeks close to His own, and said:

* Luke 11:5–10.

"To enter the kingdom of heaven you must become like one of these!"

He had taught men to call God their Father. And He was teaching them that in His Name they could pray as children of God.

It was an overwhelming idea, to treat with God as a Father.

Piety was in the heft and beam of Jewish life. In the villages of Palestine God was a reality all-pervading as air. Men and women, though they might not consciously think of Him often, not study Him professionally, or worry about His subtleties, were forever aware of the Lord. They were proud to be His people. They honored God, cherished His truth, praised and loved Him.

But, thanks to the Pharisees, it was hard for them to feel at ease with the Lord.

The Pharisees, of course, had for years been the sole experts on prayer. And their way of praying was so elaborate, so formal, that most ordinary folk confronted with children to be tended, bread to be earned and baked, with no time or money to journey often to Jerusalem, gave up before they began. The Pharisees made prayer definitely a science for the elite.

And yet hearts schooled in the reality of the One God hunger for the food of His love. These ordinary people were all children of Abraham, of Moses. The songs of David echoed in their souls. They longed to pray.

And they came to Jesus with the constant request:

"Lord, teach us how to pray."

One thing was true about this Jesus. He made prayer quite a simple business, an art even a child can master. He did not discount liturgy, the great public work of formal community prayer. He kept the Jewish feasts triumphantly, never shirked the sabbath in the synagogue. But He had come to show men how in private lives to pray.

Jesus prayed. Men had the feeling that He was, you might say, the living flesh and bone of prayer.

Even the way He stood, the power and control in Him, seemed to reach in praise like a cedar from the north country of Lebanon. His hands appeared to lift the whole world upward in consecration, as if giving thanks for everything He saw and felt. He would pray in the Temple, or in local synagogues, with disciples and sinners, at meals, in public, in private—unabashed, unself-conscious. And often, drawn by the silent Spirit, He would go apart from the others and pray, much the way a son will step aside from a gathering to speak to his father in secret.

It was at one such time when Jesus had been praying alone that a group of His disciples and followers asked Him to teach them more of the art of prayer.

His answer that day startled them. It came in the shape of a parable, the odd tale of the friend at midnight.

"Lord, teach us to pray," they had said.

And He had begun by reminding them of the prayer He had given them, the one we call the Lord's Prayer.

"Give us this day our daily bread," He said. . . . "Lead us not into temptation . . ." These things and more a man does ask of His God.

On the faces listening, earnest, scarred by sun and tears, tired beyond hope of rest, lines seemed to deepen. A man asks, *And who is to say God will answer? In His might and power, in the awesome holiness of His Name and His Kingdom, could He care about a man's daily bread?* Bread for the body, bread for the soul—all the want and emptiness of a man were caught up and pictured in the symbol of His daily bread.

Jesus saw resignation capture their faces. He smiled, startling them, turning on them the wise twinkle of a child who holds a tremendous secret.

"Suppose one of you," He said slowly, "having a friend, goes to him in the middle of the night and says to him:

"'Friend—lend me three loaves of bread, for a friend of mine has just come to me from a journey, and I have nothing to set before him to eat!'"

From His voice they could picture the man at midnight outside of the door of the house, half apologetic for disturbing one friend, half desperate for the proper entertainment of another.

"And," continued Jesus, "from inside he would answer and say:

"'Do not trouble me! The door is now shut, and my children are with me in bed. I cannot get up and give you bread!'"

With sniffs, and grunts hidden under their breath, the men smiled at the reply.

Who would want to get up in the middle of the night to lend bread? A family in these villages slept all together on pallets on the floor of the one room of their house. A man would have to step over his sleeping family, find a light, waken everyone, and most likely put up with restless cranky children the rest of the night. And what would his wife say, surrendering her own loaves for some meddlesome traveler who should manage to arrive at a more decent hour?

It was, certainly, a vivid situation. But what had it to do with prayer? Thomas scratched his heavy short beard and shrugged. It sounded like one more proof that God could not be expected to answer every prayer, no matter how well intentioned or altruistic.

But Jesus held out a warning finger, and His face grew more serious.

"I say to you—that, although he will not get up and give the bread to him because he is his friend, yet, if he will keep on knocking, because of his importunity he *will* get up and give him all he needs!"

One by one faces lifted in surprise, and in the soft laughter of amazement at this teaching about God.

Persistence! A man knocks again and again on a neighbor's door at midnight, refuses to stop asking, makes such a nuisance of himself that to be rid of him his friend will give him the three loaves. And a man, praying to God, his dearest Friend, his Father—must do the same! He must keep asking. He must, actually, be willing to make a nuisance of himself in prayer.

Thomas grinned, pulling his beard till the small dark curls snapped back softly against his chin. It is true, he thought, that there is a sort of arrogance in a man who will ask God only once, and then quit asking because his prayer is not immediately granted. A child does not ask his father only once. A child tugs at his sleeve, and dances around him begging, day after day finding new ways to ask, refusing to believe that he will not one day be answered. And Jesus has said before, thought Thomas, that we must be as simple as children. . . .

It was hardly the kind of tale a Pharisee would tell. But those who heard Jesus that day knew that the parable was no belittling humanization of God. It was meant to show men once and for all the secret of confidence and perseverance in prayer. Believe that He can answer you, realize also that you must be willing to beg without discouragement or false pride —that was what Jesus was saying.

"I say to you," continued Jesus gravely in the silence, "ask and it shall be given to you. Seek and you shall find. Knock and it shall be opened to you."

But if you do not ask, do not seek, do not knock, who will bestir himself to answer you? On earth we must ask, and pound on the door, and try with immense effort to achieve anything.

In later years men, grasping this truth of persistence in prayer, would find many ways to speak of it. Storming heaven, some would call it, a test of faith, a show of endurance.

But Jesus had said it more simply:

"Knock—and it shall be opened."

And wherever today a man must ask a favor of another, and face rebuff, and ask again—in business, by phone or letter, or standing at midnight on a neighbor's front step—the lesson in prayer that Jesus gave is repeated.

That was His way, to touch the little incidents of life and turn them into textbooks of heaven. It was the way of a man as free and simple as a child.

13

THE UNCLEAN SPIRIT THAT RETURNED*

IT WAS a sight worth a week's journey to see the tall lean figure stride out of the crowd, bend with an impact of tenderness, touch—and heal.

There were those watching who said they could almost feel the power of heaven gathering and going forth from Him. And others, standing aloof but alert, mumbled behind their fingers and wondered.

Some unearthly force was at work. There was no doubting that. An old fellow whom everyone knew—the one with the withered, emaciated hand—suddenly in full view of a packed synagogue found that hand made firm and pliant. Blind men winced and shivered at the sudden onslaught of joy and sight. A dead girl—Jairus' daughter—got up from her bed for supper while the funeral mourners still wept downstairs.

There was no hoax. Fraud and collusion were impossible. These people on whom Jesus worked His miracles were well known in town, beyond suspicion. Even the Pharisees, after discreet investigation, had to admit the cures genuine.

The problem was—how did Jesus do these things? Certainly He was no tawdry magician. No mumbo-jumbo led

* Matthew 12:43-45; Luke 11:24-26.

up to His cures. He did what He did quietly, without crescendo.

To command health and life requires more than human power. The Pharisees could not and would not believe that Jesus acted with God's power. There was only one other explanation.

The morning that He cured the blind and dumb man they said it out loud.

An ungainly, noisy, odorous caravan of the sick and the crippled and the maimed surrounded Him, people come from all over Palestine, hoping for help. And among them were some who were actual victims of diabolical possession, unwilling captives of demons and evil spirits.

Not a man in that crowd would have denied the reality of devils. Of course, the village folk were more than a little infected with the taint of the paganism of Babylon. They would assure you solemnly that every disaster from the spilling of a pot of scalding water to an old lady's toothache was caused by demons. They could offer you the best advice on charms and amulets to ward off evil spirits. Superstition had come to mar the original stark truths of Jewish faith.

But even the Pharisees and Scribes, suave and sleek in their learning, too sophisticated for blue rocks on strings or powders strewn on doorsills, knew the truth that modern men often forget. They knew that the devil and his cohorts are terribly real.

The Scribes especially were considered experts on demonology. They knew that God had created not only the earthly spheres of life—vegetable, animal, and human—but also the purely spiritual beings called angels. And they knew that some of the angels had fallen in sinful rebellion against God to become the spirits of hell.

What detail Scripture did not supply about angels and demons, the Haggadah did. The Haggadah was one of the monumental works compiled by generation after generation of Scribes, a work expanding Scripture history and doctrine with legend and patient thought. Unlike the Halakah, which covered the laws of human conduct, the Haggadah dealt almost entirely with the future and the life of the world beyond this.

And somewhere between these long-bearded speculations of the Scribes and the whispered precautions of the villagers lay the unalterable gaunt truth that devils do exist and that they can rule a man's soul by temptation or by possession.

That morning Jesus was confronted with a man possessed by a devil, blind and dumb in his agony. And Jesus bent over the man and cured him. The devil left him. And instantly he could see and speak.

The murmur of the crowd rose to a rumble and a cry:

"Can this be the Son of David? The Messiah! The Promised One!"

The Pharisees darted into the thickness of the crowd.

"This Man," they said to every ear, "casts out devils, yes! But how? By the power of Beelzebub, prince of the devils!"

They spread their warning in thick whispers of infectious fear. But Jesus knew what they were saying. And His reply came clear through the tensed air.

"If Satan casts out Satan, he is divided against himself!" He laughed. "And if I cast out devils by Beelzebub then—by whom do your own children cast them out?"

The crowds drew in their breath at this reminder. Only a short while before, Jesus had commissioned His disciples to cast out devils, and they had done so. And most of those disciples were born and bred here in Capharnaum. You could not call Peter and Andrew, or Zebedee's sons, servants of the devil! They were decent men. Everyone knew that.

Jesus smiled at the Pharisees, stretching out one hand to them as if presenting them with the only other choice.

"But then—if I cast out devils by the Spirit of God—then the kingdom of God has come upon you!"

There in the square, near the tented awnings of the pot merchants, the cloth sellers, the spice bazaars, and the sellers of sheep, Jesus taught that morning in an invisible amphitheater of silence.

And what He was teaching was the truth of the war between God and Satan, and of the choice a man must make for good or for evil.

The line was drawn in blazing fire between the Holy Spirit and the spirits of evil. And He stood as a champion stands, head high in the crowning sunlight.

"He who is not with Me is against Me," said Jesus.

And He said: "Blasphemy against the Spirit will not be forgiven."

The Scribes and the Pharisees wove their way through the quiet knots of the people till they circled Him like a fringe of oiled and perfumed elegance. They understood precisely what He was saying. He was announcing Himself as the Messiah, the One to establish the kingdom of heaven. They had no intention of letting Him do so unchallenged.

They bowed ever so slightly.

"*Master . . .*" Their voices underlined the name with irony. "We would like to see You give us a sign—a proof of Your mission."

He flung His answer like a whip through the silence.

"It is an evil and adulterous generation that seeks a sign," He said, "and no sign shall be given it but the sign of Jonas the prophet!"

In later days men would remember those words, when Jesus would, like Jonas, be swallowed up in death for three days and three nights. Now they heard only the mournful anger of His deep young voice, lamenting the fact that this generation, who had been prepared for His coming and who saw it, had not the courage to accept it.

And it was then that He told the strange parable of the unclean spirit.

"When an unclean spirit has gone out of a man," said Jesus, His eyes searching the ragged edges of the crowd for the blind and dumb man He had just cured, "then that spirit walks through dry places, seeking rest, and finds none."

Out in the wilderness, in the dry barren wastes of the hills, in caves lived the outcasts of society, madmen and lepers. There too, men knew, wandered the demons and evil spirits, lost in the wind and storm.

"Then he says," continued Jesus, "'I will return to the house I came from.' And, returning, he finds it empty—swept and adorned. Then he goes and takes with him seven other spirits more wicked than himself, and they enter in and dwell there. And the last state of that man is made worse than the first!"

He raised those dark melancholy eyes. "So," He said, "shall it be with this wicked generation also."

The parable had cast a thin sheet of horror over the faces of His listeners—over the swollen-nosed merchant, the woman with a child sleeping on her hip, over the fishermen and the farmers and the Scribes and the Pharisees. They stirred, coughing a bit, shifting their feet in the dust, shading their eyes from the suddenly hot noonday sun.

Slowly, with His help, they would find the inner meaning of that tale. They would see that Jesus was saying that no man's soul can remain empty. It is not enough for the power of evil to be evicted. The house must be ruled by one power or another.

And Jesus stood in silent prayer, holding them till they grasped the shaft of truth in that strange tale.

"He who is not with Me is against Me," He had said.

And those men and women in Capharnaum, that motley pilgrimage of the sick, understood that they must choose once and for all between good and evil, between Jesus and the devil.

A soul cannot remain empty, Jesus was saying. It cannot be its own master. It is a house that must be occupied. It must belong to God or become prey to the terror and destruction of evil. There is no middle ground of neutrality in the battle of demon against God.

Today it is not fashionable to talk of devils and unclean spirits. Modern minds are not at home with such a tale. If we were to make our own parable today we would talk perhaps in terms of psychiatry, or psychosomatic medicine, or even sociology.

But the truth does not change, even when we perfume it and camouflage it with scientific jargon. It is still not enough for us to turn evil away from our door. We may sweep our souls clean, garnish them with festoons of morality and ethics. But they must have a master.

If we do not choose to invite the Spirit of God to occupy our souls, the spirits of evil will come unasked, and take us captive before we even realize they have come.

The Pharisees had their warning, as we have ours. They did not intend to side with evil. But they would not accept Jesus. And there was no neutral ground.

"He who is not with Me is against Me." . . .

And who is to say that the tale of the unclean spirit is not a tale of life today as much as the parable of the prodigal son, or of a farmer sowing a crop? If we think there are no evil spirits today, could it be because we are also not aware of the need for the Holy Spirit in our souls?

There is nothing the devil likes better than to convince men he does not exist. He is, after all, as Scripture says, the father of lies. . . .

14

THE RICH FOOL*

He WAS bound to be misunderstood. The astounding thing was that He was so patient about it. The disciples would remember that later, and marvel.

He had come to offer men heaven, and the Pharisees labeled Him an agent of the devil. He had come to open the kingdom of grace, and people wanted instead a rebel leader to overthrow Caesar and rule a new, free state of Israel.

Even the Twelve, closer to Him than any men living, scarcely began to understand the truth for which He would die. They were waiting for heaven on earth, and were more than ready to elbow their way to the top places in it. When He spoke of suffering and death they nodded gravely, and forgot.

He was not, by the world's standards, accomplishing very much. He was working in one of the tiniest, most obscure provinces of the Empire. Even there He had to vie for attention with taxes, and the state of the weather and talk of wars, and gossip of palaces. He was a minor celebrity. But He was not understood by the very people whom God had chosen for centuries to prepare for His coming.

He was the world's most resounding failure. He con-

* Luke 12:13–21.

tained within Himself the power of creation—all wisdom, all strength, what men would one day think of as the divine secret of success. Yet He was struck with loneliness and the humiliating frustration of being misinterpreted by the world He loved.

A more sensitive heart never beat. No skin of callousness or pride protected Him from the awareness of being rejected. And for Jesus His months of public preaching were a time of daily anguish. A lesser man would have wheeled in anger to crush the world to its knees in recognition. But this was no ordinary man. And He lived as He taught, by a difficult truth —by the value of the Cross.

He had said it often enough. He said that men must not set their hearts on success in this world. He said that what men feared most—poverty, failure, suffering, death—were not important in themselves. What mattered was to do and to love the will of God, trusting in Him to take care of the outcome in His own time. If a man kept his eyes on the kingdom of God the rest would take care of itself.

And that was how He lived. He gave every heartbeat and breath to the service of His Father—preaching, teaching, healing, loving, tending the business of salvation. He met daily defeat and went on. This was, He seemed to say, the pattern for the new human life, the way that led to heaven.

To the world such a way of life would seem a waste of time. But the road in time is short, and heaven is forever. . . .

The day had dawned in a heavy fog, a thick white mist that pressed down on the low lake like a cloud of death. The wetness of the air settled into the folds of cloaks and tunics, and clung in droplets to the hair as it lay on men's shoulders. But in spite of the weather the shore of the lake had its crowd, shoving for better view of Him, heels grinding on bare toes, jostling and milling till Jesus began to speak.

He spoke that morning of hypocrisy, and of hell, and of the fear—and love—of God. Whatever you do, He said, God knows it, for you cannot hide from God. And you should know that the world is not to be feared—but only God. And then, almost without warning, He began on a new subject, the overwhelming fact that men were to find eternal life through Him.

"Whoever shall confess Me before men, him shall the Son of Man also confess before the angels of God. But he that shall deny Me before men—shall be denied before the angels of God!"

Absolute silence covered the lake. Only the trails of white fog moved, twisting silently through the masts of the beached boats.

They are really listening today, thought James. Today He is touching their hearts. . . .

The voice of Jesus moved onward, to the Holy Spirit this time, and His guidance in time of peril. *The Father. The Son. The Holy Spirit* . . . It was a time of the deepest teaching, when His hands stretched through the mist as if to reach every mind and soul.

No one moved. Not a grain of sand crunched underfoot.

And then from the crowd came a thin young man with dark rumpled hair and a sallow skin—to ask a question.

James watched him approvingly. It was a good sign when men asked questions. It showed they were grasping the message. . . .

"Master," the young man said in that solemn silence, "speak to my brother for me! He won't divide the inheritance with me. Tell him to share the money with me!"

For a long moment Jesus stared into those troubled young eyes. And then—He laughed, a long low chuckle aimed not at the lad cut out of a will but at Himself, and at the world that will not be swayed from its own thoughts.

"Man," said Jesus, "who has appointed Me judge or divider over you?"

It was a rebuke, and a kind of wry joke, an echo of Scripture that the men of Galilee would recognize. They would remember vividly that when Moses in Egypt, before the days when he spoke to God on the mountain, set himself to interfere in other men's troubles he had ended up murdering an Egyptian to save a mistreated Jew. And he got no thanks for it from the other Jews. The next day Moses had tried to stop a quarrel between two Jews, and both had turned on him with the question:

"Who appointed you prince and judge over us?"

Jesus shook His head and smiled. He had not come to be a referee. He had come to tend the mystery of the kingdom of heaven. And for answer He had a young man so worried about his own interests and resentments that he did not listen to a sermon. Well then, He would use the young man for a new sermon!

He turned to the audience on the beach.

"Be careful," He said, "and beware all covetousness—for a man's life does not consist in the abundance of things he possesses!"

And there in the damp and silence of the shore He told them the parable of the rich man who had a problem.

"There was a certain rich man," said Jesus, "whose land brought forth plenty of fruits. And he thought to himself: 'What shall I do, because I have no room to store my harvests?'"

The young man had stepped back a bit, over by the tallest date palms. He looked now at Jesus with sharp eyes, as if daring Him to make fun of him in his poverty.

But Jesus continued calmly:

"And he said: 'This is what I will do. I will pull down my barns and build greater ones. And into them I will gather all the things that have grown for me, and all my goods!'"

The people stirred. Sandals grazed on the pebbles. What kind of problem was this for a parable, the burden of a fat rich man trying to make room for his treasures? He should come to their houses. There were no storage problems in the homes of the poor!

Jesus went on, speaking again in the pompous tones of the rich man: "'And I will say to my soul: Soul, you have much treasure laid up for many years. Take your rest now. Eat, drink, and make good cheer!'"

He turned till His glance caught the young man and held it, and He continued:

"But God said to him: 'You fool, this night do they require your soul of you—and whose shall these things be that you have stored up and provided?'"

This night do they require your soul. . . . They who claim the soul that does not live with God, coming in death, unannounced, unwarned . . .

"So it is," said Jesus, "with the man who lays up treasure for himself—and is not rich toward God!"

He bowed, ever so slightly, to the young man, as if pleading to be understood for refusing to settle the problems of inheritance and treasure. And His smile was tender as a father's.

He met only a blank stare.

"Therefore," He said, turning to the Twelve nearest Him, "I say to you: Be not solicitous for your life—what you shall eat, nor for your body—what you shall put on. Consider the ravens, for they do not sow or reap, and they have no storehouse or barn—and God feeds them. How much more valuable are you than they?"

The Twelve grunted in agreement. They would understand in part, even now. They knew He did not mean for a man to ignore the right demands of the body. Why, only a week before He had by a miracle fed five thousand men and their families in the wilderness. And had He not a while later seen the discouragement of the fishermen in this same lake and shown them where to cast the net for the biggest catch of the season?

He was not asking men to be fools and pay no attention to the getting of their daily bread, thought James. He had taught them instead to ask their Father in heaven for it. And He had shown them proof of the Father's care. Yet could a man really live with no treasure but one of the soul? It was a difficult question.

Jesus, watching, bent His head. In time they would fully understand. The day would come when across the whole world men and women would practice the seemingly foolish wisdom that looked not at earth but at heaven. They would know, some of them, where the true riches lay.

Men would remember the strange tale of the rich man who sent his soul to have a good time while he tried to cope with the treasure that did not matter. And ordinary folk, families with budgets and emergencies, would begin to know and trust the providence of God, to live as His children unafraid of the world because their goal was to be ready in that night when their souls were to be assessed. There would be factory hands and office workers, and rich men too, who would understand that their true fortune grew only when it was forgotten in the service of heaven.

The young man under the palm trees turned and left, mumbling under his breath. If you asked him, the parable was all nonsense—and this Master was a coward, afraid to take a stand on anything really important, like justice.

Jesus saw him go. And, taking a breath, He turned again to those who remained.

15

THE UNSUPERVISED STEWARDS[*]

H<small>E WAS</small> a superb realist.

One look no one had ever seen on His face was surprise. He seemed to know human nature in all its nooks and crannies, in every face and form it could ever take. Disease and deformity of the body, festers and twists of the soul He met with sadness and with love—but never with shock.

Peter had heard it said that if a man looked deeply enough into his own heart he could know all hearts. But Jesus was no ordinary man. Flesh and blood, mind and soul, He was supremely human. But He was also the Christ, the Son of the living God. Peter had called Him that, moved by a Spirit he could not understand—and by that name Peter had touched truth. The fiery shiver of that touch had never left him.

What baffled him was that the Christ, Who was supremely without sin, should understand so well the weakness of other men. It was like suggesting that a man in perfect health should be able, by examining his own body, to grasp the cause and cure of every possible illness. How could He know?

But John and Andrew remembered their first sight of Jesus —and they understood. They had been that day with John the Baptist in the thick green air of the Jordan's banks, when

[*] Matthew 24:45–51; Luke 12:40–48.

Jesus came out of the wilderness. Forty days He had been there alone, forty days of fasting and prayer, and at the end of that time He had met the devil himself. John and Andrew had seen His face. They could not doubt that in that desert Jesus had grappled with the utmost power of temptation, and triumphed.

He knew the bald face of evil. He had felt the subtle claws of the tempter's deception on His soul. Because He was human He knew the battle each man must enter, the single-handed combat to be won by grace and will. And, being neither a cynic nor a naïve idealist, He warned every soul He met that it might be caught off guard and vanquished.

It is exasperating, when you are on fire with a dream of perfection, to be told to be wary of faltering on the way. The young lover does not believe there are future quarrels to be weathered. The soul young in grace shrinks from the mention of sin. Pride weaves its way through the loftiest visions.

And Jesus had no time or patience for pride. He stood, feet braced in broad stance, eyes unflinching, and warned His Twelve and all who would come after them to be vigilant night and day.

He warned of three things: the destruction of Jerusalem, the end of the world, and the end of each man's life on earth.

To the Twelve, at the time, the three seemed intermingled, bound together in the foreboding of disaster, in omens and signs and terrors. Yet the three were not the same. And the one He spoke of most often was the moment of death, the hour of reckoning for each soul.

Death would come swiftly and secretly as a thief in the night. A man might be working the field, a woman grinding grain, eating, drinking, marrying, caught in the high tide of daily affairs. And suddenly for him time would end and eternity begin. Christ Himself would come to judge that soul.

"Keep watch!" He said. "Because you do not know what hour your Lord will come."

He said: "Keep your loins girded, and lamps burning in your hands."

He reminded them that no home would ever be burglarized if the man of the house knew at what hour the thief planned to come. He told them that the master of an estate would bless the servants he found ready for him when he came home unannounced from a wedding.

And the Twelve grew restless with such tales. They could not imagine themselves caught napping in the hour of judgment. Surely they were too close to Him to be trapped into laziness or callousness. They had put sin behind them forever. Did He really believe they were capable of betraying His trust?

It was Peter finally who asked: "Lord—do you speak this parable to us? Or for all men?"

Jesus had been resting under a ledge of rock, eating with the others a lunch of cheese and of figs from Nathanael's mother's yard. Now He sat forward, the shadow of the stone slashing across His earnest brow. And, looking at Peter, He told a new parable, the tale of the unsupervised stewards.

"Who, do you think," He began, "is the faithful and wise steward whom his lord sets over his family to give them their measure of grain at the proper time? Blessed is the servant whom the master, when he comes, shall find so doing! Truly, I say to you, he will set him over all he possesses."

Peter tugged at his ear and blinked. Such a steward had been entrusted with a position of real importance. It was a serious responsibility to manage the storehouses and supplies wisely in the master's absence, to care for a whole household. Such a job well done would deserve great reward.

And, since Jesus was looking directly at him, Peter thought

perhaps he was to be that steward. Peter would not have said so out loud, but privately he felt that he could be trusted to handle matters as the Master would wish. . . .

Jesus, watching Peter, bowed His head as if in prayer. Then carefully He continued:

"But if that servant shall say in his heart: 'My master is a long time coming'?"

A long time coming—there was the thorn. Here in Palestine a rich man could leave on a journey meant to last a month and be gone three years. It took a staunch steward to supervise himself in such an absence.

Anyone can be faithful for a short while. The knowledge that any moment the master will return keeps a man on his toes. But even for the best of men the first fervor of responsibility will dull to drudgery. The sense of power can make a man giddy. . . .

"And if he shall begin to strike the menservants and the maidservants, and to eat and to drink, and be drunk?"

The Twelve nodded sadly. They had all seen stewards grow ugly and debauched when left alone too long in a position of trust. There was the overseer of that estate on the hill in Capharnaum, for example. He had meant well. But as time passed he had begun to take one small liberty after another, to forgive himself one fault after another. A little self-indulgence, a fit of temper—and the next day another, with no one to praise or blame. He had ended in disgrace.

"Then," said Jesus, "that servant's master will come in the day he least hopes to see him, and at the hour he does not know—and shall separate him, and give him his reward with the unbelievers!"

That last phrase caught in their ears, sudden reminder that this was after all not just a commentary on human behavior, not gossip but a parable—a teaching from which they themselves were to learn a lesson.

Was it for them He painted the garish contrast between the steward who passed the test and the one who did not? Could He mean it as warning for them?

He did. There was no doubt of that. Peter could read those eyes as surely as he read the storm signs in the color of the lake waters. And what he saw in that face chilled him with fear.

His cheeks flushed red with shame as he realized that he had fooled himself but not his Master. Jesus knew his strength and his faults, the hidden weakness through which temptation would enter, the danger that lay in wait for Peter. And because He loved him He warned him.

In that moment Peter suddenly understood that humility and realism are but two names for the same wisdom.

Jesus designed the parable for him, Peter knew. And for all the Twelve. He meant it for Christians of all time, for the realists who are willing to face the fact that they can be either saint or sinner, hero or failure in the long-drawn-out siege that is life.

Every instant, thought Peter, a man must be armed—against the devil, against himself. And the most powerful weapon a man could have was clear sight of humility, and the awareness that when the time seems longest it is short.

He sighed. The picture of the two unsupervised stewards seemed painted in fire on his mind. It was a tale he prayed he would never forget. It was a parable of his own life, a story with two possible endings. And until the moment of death he would not be sure which he had made his own.

16

THE FACE OF THE SKY*

HE SWUNG down from the prow, landing neatly and nimbly on the shore, running with the others to pull on the ropes, beaching the boat away from the insistent lure of the waves.

They sang as they worked, coiling the ropes, washing the deck with heavy skins of water. He sang with them, His tunic girded high around His legs to free Him for work.

He looked like a man on a holiday, exulting in sudden freedom. The scarlet sunset beginning behind the town filtered into a pale red dust on the swell of the water. The cool of the evening rose around the thirteen men like fragrance.

They had not been alone together for a long time. Crowds had dogged their trail, hounding them around the lake, insisting on more preaching, more cures. And the pressure of people, of voices and constant demands, had worn on them all like the rubbing of pebbles against each other under the waves.

They had at last sailed back across the lake. The small voyage had been like a floating island of silence, comforting them, holding them all in the cradle of movement. Now, ashore again, they burst out like children restored.

* Matthew 16:2–4; Luke 12:54–57.

A man can have too much of miracles. Even God rested on the seventh day. . . .

They were not to rest long. The town of Capharnaum had been eating its supper, gathered by its firesides and cookpots in peace. But a delegation now proceeded past the synagogue down to the shore, a group whose sophistication called for later dinner hours and immediate attention to business at hand.

He saw them coming. In the gloaming they marched like figures from a pagan frieze, solemn, ritualistic, and exquisitely disapproving.

Pharisees and Sadducees together—the two warring forces of Jewish faith joining hands to come against Him! Jesus smiled wryly. Nothing but common peril could make them walk side by side.

The Sadducees were the priestly aristocracy, richer far than the Pharisees, concerned not with quibbles over morality and faith but with keeping a firm grip on the power and fortune that came with control of the Temple. If you insisted on talking religion you would find the Sadducees more fundamentalist than the Pharisees. They took the word of God as it was found in Scripture with none of the elaborate oral tradition so dear to the Pharisees' hearts. If it was not spelled out in the Holy Writ, then the Sadducees were not interested.

The Pharisees thought the Sadducees were soulless clods growing fat on the piety of good men. The Sadducees thought the Pharisees were fanatics, hypocrites who only wished they could hold the reins of power. Theologically, they differed on such matters as the existence of angels, of divine providence, and the resurrection of the body. Practically, they hated each other's noses.

But they marched shoulder to shoulder to the lake shore that evening in complete agreement. Jesus of Nazareth threatened the comfortable structure of their faith—and their power.

They came because they had heard quite terrifying and obviously exaggerated stories of what had happened on the other side of the water this afternoon. A miracle of impossible proportions was supposed to have occurred—the feeding of four thousand families with only seven loaves of bread and a few little fishes. It was even claimed that after the crowds had their fill there were whole basketfuls of leftovers gathered up!

They came to examine and discredit the credentials of this Messianic pretender. They found Him singing and working like a common fisherman—without dignity or purpose. If it were not that the people were enchanted by Him they would not have wasted breath or run the risk of getting sand in their shoes. But . . .

"We have come . . ." they began.

Jesus nodded, and sprang to greet them as if He were a properly robed rabbi welcoming disciples into his study.

". . . we have come to see if you can give us a sign from heaven!"

The silence stretched till it embarrassed them. Behind Him the Twelve stopped their work, sitting like misplaced figure-heads on the boat to listen. In front of Him the Pharisees and Sadducees, their hair and turbans edged with sunset glow, stared unsteadily back at that long, powerful face.

A sign? He knew what sign they wanted. It was said, in tradition, that the Messiah would duplicate the great mira-cles of the days of Moses—especially that He, like Moses, would feed the children of Israel with manna from heaven.

Obviously the news of the feeding of the thousands, the actual multiplication of the substance of bread and fish, had traveled to their ears. Obviously, too, they did not believe the report this time, any more than they had believed the news of the first such miracle, when He had fed five thousand families with only four loaves and two fishes.

They would not have believed it if they had seen it and eaten of it themselves. They would have called it a trick, an example of mass hypnosis, of general hallucination. They could not afford to believe in such a miracle!

The foremost of the Sadducees, a round-bellied little man with sideburns that plunged into the depths of his beard, repeated in imperious tones:

"A sign—that is all we ask for. But if You cannot give it . . . ?"

The evening meal was over. Capharnaum had left its supper bowls to capture the twilight breeze. In twos and threes it seemed that the whole town was drifting to the shore. And, seeing the strange array of men by Peter's boat, they came to listen and to watch.

Then Jesus spoke—and, as so often before, He wrapped His answer in the trappings of every day, in a parable of the signs of weather in the sky.

"When it is evening," He began, raising a long pointed finger to the ecstasy of sunset behind His challengers, "you say: 'The sky is red, and so there will be fair weather.'

"And in the morning: 'Today there will be a storm, for the sky is red and lowering.'"

He smiled, ingratiating, simple as a fisherman Himself. The delegation frowned. Like all city men, they took a certain pride in knowing the lore of the country. They wore folk knowledge like a badge to prove they had not lost the common touch. It made a man feel wise to be able to look at the sky and repeat the old adages and find them coming true. There's a ring around the moon, a Sadducee would say as he peered from a Temple porch—and that means a storm. The clouds lie like the scales of a fish, a Pharisee would say as he walked contentedly through the narrow streets of Jerusalem, and that means rain for the crops. . . .

It was the borrowed truth of the men of the sea and the soil they quoted, as little a part of their own lives as curios in a shelf.

Jesus bowed ever so slightly and went on:

"When you see a cloud rising from the west, you soon say: 'A shower is coming'—and it happens.

"And when you see the south wind blow, you say: 'There will be heat'—and it comes to pass."

He flung His head upward till His eyes searched the sky for the first sign of stars. Behind Him the waves lapped quicker on the stones, as if to hasten the approach of night.

"You hypocrites," He said, and His voice was low and sad as the evening wind. "You know how to discern the face of heaven and of the earth. Then how is it that you do not discern this time?"

He opened His hands slightly in the dusk, and it seemed that the last glow of day centered and drew itself to surround Him as He moved forward to confront them with His answer.

"You know how to read the face of the sky. And can you not know the signs of the times?"

His words hung like a warning in the dusk.

And on that shore were those who remembered the signs—the coming of John the Baptist, the working of miracles, the feeding of the people in the wilderness. Some few there were who remembered even further back, to the tales their parents told, of how some thirty years ago strange lights had filled the heavens, and magi had journeyed from the east, and there had been talk of a new King born in Israel.

There were signs aplenty for those who could see them and were willing to read them. A storm did not come with a herald to announce it in so many words. The good weather of to-morrow did not shout its coming the night before. Nor did the Messiah blare forth His arrival with proclamations. A man must use his eyes and ears, and read the signs of the times, or else take what comes, unprepared.

The lore of weather was not born and bred into Pharisees and Sadducees. The lore of Scripture was. If they were indeed at home in the country of the spirit, steeped in the rhythm of God's truth, then surely they would have known.

The fact that they did not was a rebuke forever.

The people of the lake town looked up to the sky where the first stars hung like beacons to heaven. The Pharisees and the Sadducees looked at each other.

Jesus, with His Twelve, went His way through the darkness, unseen and unnoticed except by those who knew a sign when they saw one.

Still today men say:

> "*Red sky at night, sailor's delight.*
> *Red sky in the morning, sailors take warning.*"

The signs of weather do not change. Nor do the signs of the arrival of Christ and His teaching. The problem is to know how and where to look for the marks of God on earth.

17

THE MUSTARD SEED *

I T W A S really a most unimpressive show.

There was this carpenter from Nazareth, of all places, who apparently simply quit work to tramp the roads teaching. He made His pulpit where He happened to be—on a rock, on a street corner, or as on this day in a slightly odorous fishing boat. His robe and turban were only workaday clothes, without any fancy trappings.

And the men with Him, twelve of them, were even less distinguished than He—a band of young vagrants without visible means of support. Four of them were born right here on the lake—fishermen and sons of fishermen—Peter and his brother Andrew, James and his brother John.

And this particular day the four were struck with a secret self-consciousness, a kind of embarrassment for themselves and for Him. Ridiculous as it seemed, they had a hankering to lend Jesus and themselves a touch of grandeur—a procession, perhaps, or a fine set of robes—something to impress the townsfolk.

Really, thought Peter and Andrew, this is a most undistinguished beginning for the Master. He seems to have no sense of the fitness of things. He speaks of the kingdom of

* Matthew 13:31–32; Mark 4:30–34; Luke 13:18–19.

heaven. But who will believe Him or us if He goes around looking like a beggar instead of a king? And why, if He is all that He says, doesn't He launch this crusade properly? How about the legions of angels that sang at His birth? Where are they now?

It was not, truly, that they craved pomp and display for themselves. Even the attention they did receive now made them uncomfortable. But they were so convinced of the momentous significance of this work of Jesus that they yearned to stage it properly for the whole world to see and understand.

Besides, it is a little difficult to keep faith in the midst of such unpromising, unimpressive circumstances. Change earth and represent heaven with a group like this? It was, thought Andrew, about as impossible as sweeping this beach clean of shells with only a gull feather for a broom.

Peter nudged his brother with a blunt elbow and pointed to the crowd. They clustered around the beached ship where Jesus spoke, along the scalloped line of the waves, up the graveled shore and over the wall—hundreds listening.

Something held these men and women, the skeptical, worldly, laughing people of Capharnaum. Something more intimately powerful than fine words or fiery show gripped them in absolute silence. No personal magnetism could explain it. And as for His message, He was speaking now in parables, little cryptograms that would surely puzzle some of His listeners.

What was it, then, that gave Him this power over an audience?

At that same moment Jesus leaned His long callused hands on the prow of the fishing boat and bent to look directly at His Twelve, as if in answer.

"The kingdom of heaven," He said, "is like a grain of mustard seed!"

In spite of himself, Andrew sighed. Parables were drawn from such exasperatingly small things, and of seeds he had heard enough. There had been the sower and the seed, and the cockle among the grain. And now—a mustard seed.

"Like a mustard seed," said Jesus, "which a man took and planted in his field. It is indeed the smallest of all seeds, the least among them."

Perhaps botanists know of smaller seeds, but everyone on that shore knew that the pale brown mustard seed was so tiny you could lose it under your fingernail. About the size of a speck of ground pepper it was, pungent, spicy—and far too much of a nuisance to be planted individually.

"But," said Jesus, "when it grows, it is greater than the other herbs. It becomes—a tree!"

He waved a hand at the hills of wilding running down to the shore. And the people turned and looked as if for the first time at the mustard bushes growing there. There were the ordinary black mustards, with their yellow flowers and notched seed pods. They grew a good twelve feet tall, twice the height of a man. And then there were what we would call toothbrush trees, not real mustards but spicy-seeded, whose twigs were tied together and used to clean teeth.

From a speck to a tree—it was, come to think of it, amazing!

"And the birds of the air," said Jesus, "come and live in the branches of that tree."

The birds of the air shall come—it was a familiar phrase in Israel. Ezekiel the prophet had had a vision of the Messiah and of His age as a small tree growing till the birds from all corners of the earth should come and dwell in it. Up in the synagogue, within sight of this shore, those Scriptures were read to the men of Capharnaum. And here by the lake Jesus was saying:

"The kingdom of heaven is like a mustard seed"—growing to be a tree to shelter and welcome the birds of the air.

Insignificant, Peter? Unimpressive? Indeed—these years of preaching, of suffering and death, will seem as worthless as a mustard seed, lost in the sight of men, falling unnoticed into the ground of history. That is the way it should be, must be.

The seed, that tiny dot in your hand, holds within it a power unseen and unknown, a power placed there by God. Drop it, forget it. It will find its own way to grow. With the indomitable will of God it will grow, pushing aside rocks, thrusting its way upward in obedience to His plans. The seed you scorned contains the secret of life, and it will grow to ten million million times its original size.

And that is the way it is to be with the kingdom of heaven, with the Church on earth, Peter. It also contains the secret of God's own life, the creative force of grace. It is planted here in Palestine, unseen and unnoticed. And it will grow to cover the whole earth.

Peter would live to see the first startling growth of the faith. In the years ahead he and the other apostles would learn first hand the quiet workings of this power of grace. Like their Master, they would begin their work in obscurity. Peter's church in Rome would be an undercover thing, a nuisance to the proper authorities of the Empire, even as a weed is to a proper gardener. But the church would contain the surging power to rise up through the stone of indifference, to overcome persecution, and triumph.

Peter, Andrew, James, John, Thomas, all of you—the Master was saying—you are most unimpressive men in yourselves, even as I. You will be nothing in the world's eyes while you

live. Neither am I. There will be times when your own little-
ness will appall you, when you will wonder why I have chosen
you, and why, since I have chosen you, I do not dignify you
with a show of glory. The world will take care of that, in time.
The grown tree is decked in flowers. The seed is plain, husk-
brown, and ugly.

Even today, nearly two thousand years after that afternoon
on Capharnaum's shore, the kingdom is not yet full grown.
And most of us who serve Him are quite as insignificant in the
sight of the world as a mustard seed. Our work in the world
is as nothing—a prayer, a small kindness, the monotonous
day-to-day business of virtue.

There are times when it is very hard to believe that anything we do with and for Christ is of value—here and now, or
later. The kingdom is agonizingly slow to come, and it has
not even an overture to announce it. It is truly a test of faith,
this humbleness of Christ.

Christ could have been born in a palace. He chose an
animal's cave. He could have worked many more miracles,
have swooped in angel-winged glory from one corner of the
earth, striking men dead with His lightning, conjuring mag-
nificence to dazzle the eyes of both poor and rich. He chose
to work as a craftsman for most of His life, turning out plow
handles and stools and ladders and tables to suit the demands
of the townsmen of Nazareth. He went forth when it was time
to preach, and He worked His miracles with astute and divine
economy, each one serving an eternal purpose. He died a
shameful death, executed for a crime He did not and could
not commit—the crime of blasphemy tagged to the Son of
God.

He chose the little way. We can say, and it is true, that
He chose the way of obscurity because He came to show us
how to live and sanctify our own lives, which must be led

not in palaces with angels but in rooms with human beings.

But He chose the way of obscurity and poverty also because that way is the only way, the divine way of accomplishing great things.

If you did not know how God did do things, it might seem quite reasonable for Him to plant each tree of the earth full-blown with an angelic choir to sing an anthem in its honor. But God chose instead to rely on a seed, made by Him in silence.

If there were a man who had never seen or heard of the world beyond an indoor cell, how could you tell him that if you planted a speck of deadness it would become a tree taller than he? You cannot dig in the soil to see the seed grow. You would destroy it with your trowel. And the seed cannot grow except in the secrecy and darkness of the soil.

Of the hundreds who stood in the lake breeze to hear Him in Capharnaum that day, how many names do you know? The Twelve—eleven in glory, one in infamy. The shadowy imprints of a few others—a rich man named Jairus who had a daughter, a Roman centurion. The rest are lost to fame, as forgettable as a mustard seed—even as you and I.

But the kingdom grew through them. It still grows, through you and me.

18

THE LEAVEN IN THE BREAD*

WOMEN loved Him. And no man could guess why.

He was not handsome at all. He did not swagger like a Roman centurion or dazzle the eye like a silk peddler from a Far Eastern caravan. He did not play on their sympathies like a beggar. The tales of the bazaar storytellers were far more romantic than any of His.

Yet they loved Him. They would leave their jugs at the well and go to watch Him as He came quietly down the street. They would leave their cooking and weaving to trudge hours around the Lake of Galilee to listen to Him.

It was as if they knew that He held the secret spirit and substance of life. They were drawn to Him in utter truth—as simply and honestly as if hearing Him were the natural and supreme duty of their day.

The men of Capharnaum, of Jericho, of Bethany, of small towns and big, were confused and puzzled by the way He greeted their women. Everyone knew a woman's place was firmly in the home. Women were not expected to go to public meetings. Even in the synagogue a woman did not speak. The important things of life—religion, politics, and business —could be understood only by men.

* Matthew 13:33; Luke 13:20–21.

And yet women followed this Jesus, and He did not seem to find it either odd or remarkable. They behaved themselves. Even the stoniest man had to admit there was none of the atmosphere of pagan military camps or festival about this business. The women stayed in the background. But they did act as if they had some special right to be near Him and with Him.

And Jesus talked to them as if He expected them to understand. At times it even seemed that He hoped for more from them than from the men. And though He spoke most often to men in terms of men's life—of farming and soldiering, of fishing and building—there were moments when He bent His thought directly to the lives of their wives.

It seemed that He wanted to be doubly certain that a truth would not be lost. When He told the men the parable of the shepherd and the lost sheep He followed it quickly with the parable of the woman who lost a coin and cleaned house furiously till she found it.

And this day in Capharnaum He told the parable of the mustard seed and followed it with a slender parable no woman could ever forget.

He raised His head till the sunlight fell full on His deep brow and, looking up to the wall and slopes above the shore where the townswomen clustered in silence, He said:

"The kingdom of heaven is like leaven——"

Like yeast? The women smiled a little uncertainly. What could there be about such a simple thing as yeast to make one think of heaven?

Jesus continued, "—which a woman took and hid in three measures of meal. . . ."

Three measures! That would be a great deal of meal, about a bushel in our measurement. That dough would make enough bread for many families!

But Jesus said simply:

"And then the whole of it was leavened!"

The kingdom of heaven, a bit of leaven, and a basket of meal—what had they to do with each other? The men on the shore crunched the rough sand under their feet and peered out at the lake and sniffed the quickening breeze. It was a silly thing, this talk of leaven and dough, they thought.

But the women understood. In that one sentence they had caught and held a truth that would never die.

Even the oldest of them, hands browned and wrinkled by years of grinding grain in a hand mill, of pounding dough and tending ovens, could remember as a child the sense of surging mystery surrounding the baking of bread. To take a tiny bit of yeast—about one part of yeast to sixteen of meal was the custom—and mix it till it was truly hidden in the grain. To watch the dough swell and grow with a life of its own, to double in size, light and airy . . . It was one of the gentle delights of womankind then as now, a thing never quite taken for granted, part of the sweet-smelling magic of every day.

And what, after all, was this leavening? A mold, you might say, a fungus, a living plant, one cell in size, unattractive and useless-seeming as anything could be. Yet look what it did! Even a man knew the difference between the flat tasteless hardened paste of a Passover matzoth cracker compared to the thick richness of a loaf of leavened bread!

And the kingdom of heaven on earth was like the leaven hidden in the bushel of flour.

The women nodded. Yeast has a life of its own, contagious, transforming everything it touches. So too do the followers of Christ, the children of the kingdom. They hold the impulse of divine life with which to transform the world.

Men had grumbled that this Jesus did not flaunt His power

across the face of the earth. They could not see why He chose to teach in obscurity and poverty, almost unnoticed and unknown.

To answer them He had told the parable of the tiny mustard seed, lost in the ground till it grew through its God-given power into a tree.

And to answer the women He had told the parable of the leaven.

Nothing was more obscure, more humble than yeast. And yet, once mixed with the lump of dough, it will not be overcome. You cannot unleaven a batter!

The women understood. They were themselves used to obscurity. Men might be tormented with ambition, inflamed with the yearning to march in glory through the streets. Women then could not afford ambition. Their life was walled in by the well, the market, and the synagogue, centered in the home. Yet they knew that their own influence reached beyond the whitened walls of their homes, past the roof where figs dried in the sun, or the downstairs room shared with the animals. A woman walked abroad in her men. Her husband and her sons carried with them unaware the imprint of her thoughts and hopes and dreams. They knew the subtle influence of a silent belief, expressed only in small deeds, hidden in the veil of modesty and humility.

It was for men to do and for women to be—perhaps that was the way of it, they thought. The men will lead and speak and battle and conquer, spending themselves in action. The women will watch and wait and pray, filling themselves in silence. And together they will change the world.

Things are not quite the same now in our world. Women can and do take their place in the fields that were once masculine—in science, in politics, even in war. But it is still true that the power of a woman's life and love, hidden away in the home, cannot be excelled.

Today, in our cities, few women still bake their daily bread. The wonder of yeast is not part of a girl's childhood memories. We need a cookbook to tell us how to set the loaves to rise, how to punch them down to half size and let them rise again.

The women of Palestine could go to their homes and each day's chore would remind them of Jesus' words, of the kingdom of heaven and the secret glory of following Him. But what are we to do, who have given up our right to the alchemy of heaven? Where shall we find our parable?

We could think of the leaf of lavender sachet in a corner of a drawer, spreading its perfume to everything that comes near it. We could think of the drop of bluing in the wash water, whitening the clothes. But dried leaves and bluing have no life of their own. And they cannot give life and power to other things. So half the parable is lost.

We could think of a germ or virus passing unnoticed in the air, carrying the deadly power of disease to overmaster a human being incomparably larger than it. But a germ has the power of death and destruction. And the leavening of grace works for good.

We could think of penicillin, the wonder drug that has come from the mold on bread, possessing the power to conquer the evil of disease. Or the grain of radium that can activate a hundred million atoms. But penicillin and radium are not part of the rhythm of our everyday lives, the feel and smell of our daily work. They are the products of laboratories, of technical skill, not of a woman busy in her home.

We are grown too sophisticated for the parable, too far from the homely truths that Jesus learned in Mary's kitchen. We must pray that our souls do not also grow too far from the roots of divine life, that we do not live with manufactured substitutes for the bread of the spirit, produced in assembly lines, vitamin-enriched, protected against parable truth.

For we are still the yeast hidden in God's world, the silent possessors of the life that can leaven the whole.

The apostles would march like soldiers across the known world, braving persecution and hatred and death to plant the banners of the kingdom and teach His truth. Their names would live in history.

But the women would not be forgotten, either. Not Mary, His mother. Nor the Magdalene. Nor Martha, who cooked His dinners before He raised her brother Lazarus from the grave. Nor Salome, nor Susanna, nor Lydia.

They did not preach to governors. They were not stoned or jailed or martyred. But they loved Him. And then, like the living leaven, their love passed its power to others, inflaming them, lifting them to Him. It was the women who walked the way of the cross with Him, women who stood by in His agony, who buried Him. And it was to the women that the glory of His resurrection was first revealed.

The kingdom of heaven is like that.

19

THE SEED THAT GROWS BY ITSELF[*]

HE ALMOST never walked in a straight line. He would decide to sail across the lake, then hurry back as if to keep a secret appointment. He would preach one tremendous sermon in a town and never return, perform an astonishing miracle in an obscure village and never set foot there again. He camped in Capharnaum for months, then suddenly took off on an apparently aimless journey in Perea, east of the Jordan.

He could not spend one day efficiently, as men measure efficiency. He would spend an hour talking about angels to ragamuffin children, three or four minutes with an important Pharisee, half an hour on a sermon, and five hours walking to the top of a mountain and down again, alone. He would come for supper, grass-stained, wind-blown, and smiling, with a discourse on the way to do penance.

He was not systematic. He was, as far as the Twelve could see, almost careless, casual as a child, irresponsible as a man in love. He made a most unusual teacher.

Rabbis, when they taught, began with an outline, traveling slowly and carefully from point to point. That was the way James preferred. James was a man of detail and precision,

[*] Mark 4:26–29.

the kind who enjoyed unknotting and salvaging cord, and exploring tiny side tangles of argument.

Other teachers more informal, the ones considered profound and spiritual, taught with "sayings"—well-polished graceful little sentences about anything from the wetness of water to the greatness of God. Each saying was an ornament for which a disciple must make his own connecting thread. Philip liked sayings. He had as a very young man enjoyed long solitary ambles on the far shore of the lake, stopping to dream over the way of birds in the sky or the meaning of veins in a leaf.

But Jesus was not one to sit in the shade of a tree and ruminate on epigrams. And He was not one to conduct an orderly course in religion, ethics, philosophy, or metaphysics.

He would start to talk about the way to treat an enemy, find Himself explaining the art of prayer, and end up discussing divine providence, all in half an hour. The deepest subjects He would touch as casually as a field flower. He would speak of the Holy Spirit, of God the Father, then leap into a warning of persecutions to come.

When you thought about it later, the Twelve decided, it seemed haphazard, exasperating, confusing. The more you tried to sort things out in your mind, the more it seemed you had only a handful of splintered pottery, a puzzle of small shiny colored pieces.

And yet, when you listened, each word He spoke seemed to contain all truth. Even the smallest fragment seemed to lie in the soul like a gift, entire.

It was Simon the Zealot, who seldom said much, who came the closest to describing it. It seemed to him that each word was like wine. If you tasted only one drop you tasted the whole cupful—and drop by drop you could drain the cup till it was yours completely.

And there were some of the Twelve—James and John, Andrew and Peter, Philip and Nathanael—who had been with Jesus at that wedding in Cana when He changed the potfuls of water into wine. That had been the beginning of the miracles. And in a way it seemed the beginning of His teaching too. They did not contradict Simon.

But they were still puzzled. They could not believe there was no system in His truth, that they were to use only their hearts, close their eyes and brains, and follow Him blithely.

They had their answer one day in Capharnaum when He preached again by the water. The crowd that noon was so enormous that the disciples had to boost Him high on the fishing boat and push it out into the water to make a little stage from which He could speak. Then, panting slightly, their wet legs and sandy feet glistening in the sun, the Twelve had hoisted themselves aboard to listen.

A stranger coming unaware on that shore might have thought the crowd gathered to watch some impossible rescue out in the waves. Every eye focused on the Man in the ship. Every word traveled clear across the water, in the natural auditorium of the lake bowl.

No record was kept of those who came to hear Him. No collection was taken up of coins or of names. It had occurred to Nathanael that an orderly man should at least occasionally take informal census of the audience, to see which were only passers-by and which came regularly to learn more. How else could anyone follow up those who needed help, or weed out the stragglers? But Jesus had no interest in such things. He spoke for all to hear. Let those who would, listen.

And that noontide, as the boat rocked comfortably on the tiny waves, He told the parable that answered their unspoken concern, the story of the seed that grows by itself.

"The kingdom of heaven," He said, "is as if a man should

cast a seed into the earth—and then should sleep and rise, night and day, and the seed should spring up and grow while he does not know it!"

On the shore the people listened, mystified but attentive. On the boat, sitting at His feet, the Twelve turned careful eyes on their Master.

A man, after all, does not ordinarily plant a seed and then forget to take care of it. Such indifference was hardly a trait to be admired. A child may make a garden and then walk off and ignore it all summer. But a farmer would find himself hungry and homeless if he behaved that way.

James looked uneasily at his brother Jude. Jude bent his head, brushing a piece of dried sand from his ankle.

Jesus turned slightly, His hands seeming to bind the Twelve to Him, and continued, His strong voice spanning the waters:

"For by itself the earth brings forth the fruit. First the blade, then the ear, then the full grain in the ear."

He paused, as if giving time for summer growth, for grain pushing through the earth and ripening in the sun. Then he said:

"And when the fruit is ready, then immediately he puts in the sickle because the harvest has come!"

It made a strange picture, this tale of a man letting seed fend for itself till he came to gather the harvest. The people on the shore saw a field tangled with weeds, pestered by crows and rodents, a disgrace to the neighborhood—a lazy man's way to farm!

And yet, as they watched the figure in the prow of the boat, they caught a truth they had forgotten—a mystery grown dusty with everyday knowledge.

A seed does grow without man's help. Once it is in the dark dampness of the earth it will grow—not because a man tends it but because God Himself has placed in it the power and the need to grow. It has no choice but to pierce the earth, unfurl its leaves, and ripen.

A man may make life easier for the seed, may ease the soil and remove the weeds. But the seed will grow of itself. And the power in it will drive it to perfection of harvest. It had been that way since the beginning of time. It would always be that way.

And on that shore the farmers who listened realized that all the wonderful technical improvements of agriculture, all the modern advances of which they were so proud, could not in themselves make one seed grow. Though camel wheels irrigated the land, though new plows were more efficient than the old, still only God made the seed grow, hidden in the earth.

James, hugging his bony knees, stared at the greenery of the beach. Who tended the date palms towering over men's heads, there where sand met earth? Who weeded for the wild fig trees, for the berry bushes, the mustard plants? The world was covered with plants growing untended except by God, in magnificent disorder, so inefficient, so unorganized that they endured for centuries. . . .

No system? No organization? Philip grinned at his own blindness. Men would spend their lives studying and exploring the system of a plant, outlining the whole science of botany. As centuries passed men would advance to the wonders of plant chemistry, of photosynthesis, of the physics of osmosis. The day would come when the study of by-products of plant life would expand to revolutionize medicine and industry. You could study a leaf forever, and find it forming a perfect, coherent, giant web of truth. And all of that truth is held in one seed, falling by God's hidden design to live by His power.

Philip cocked his thin face till he saw only Jesus' profile

against the blue sky. And he thought that Jesus was now going through the world as God might have gone at creation, spreading the seed of the future in one small field, impelling a whole new world to grow of itself with the power of the Spirit. It would grow as Eden grew, not in neat anxious furrows, not with the sweat of a man's brow, but in the luxuriant freedom of grace, obeying the wordless command of God.

Time enough later for a science to unravel theology for men by outline and detail. The seed must grow before you can study the veins of its leaves. Time enough later for organization and husbandry. You must know what plant you are tending before you can see how to protect and strengthen it. . . .

The power of life was wrapped in every word He spoke. What matter if they did not see the pattern of His sowing? The seeds of the world are carried by the wind or by the fleet running beasts, scattered a thousand ways. Some even lie forgotten to sprout years later. And some are planted by men with loving arduous care.

Jesus smiled at His Twelve. He would change the subject again, almost at once. He would not spell out the truth then in patient scrolls. The science of Christianity could wait for another day, till the true Vine had grown by the power of the Spirit. Now was the time of seeding, of the planting of grace and truth in the good ground of their souls.

He turned and cast another parable across the water to the shore.

20

THE CHILDREN WHO WOULD NOT PLAY*

Under other circumstances they might even have liked Him.

Some of the older Pharisees felt a stirring in their hearts when they heard Him, but they mistrusted their hearts. He was too young, unsound, scandalously flighty for a man of God. They saw the joy and freedom of Him, and yearned to follow Him, and they did not dare.

The younger Pharisees were of two minds. Some, the lean earnest ones with youth's hunger for challenge, wrote Him off as too easygoing for their blood. A rabbi who went to dinner parties and spiced sermons with tales was not their idea of a proper spiritual guide. On the other hand, some of the young ones actually thought Him stodgy. They wanted someone to turn the world upside down. He seemed content to take the world as it was and remake it slowly.

He did not please them. They folded their arms and watched, waiting for Him to woo them to His side.

And Jesus walked and worked among them as if He did not care what they thought of Him. At times He looked at them

* Matthew 11:16–19; Luke 7:31–35.

with the patient, almost quizzical smile of a man who has prepared a suprise that has not yet been discovered.

One thing especially baffled the Pharisees, and that was the connection between this Jesus and John the Baptist.

They were the two most notorious religious phenomena of the time, and two more drastically different holy men could not be imagined. They were, oddly enough, cousins. John was only a few months older than Jesus. They were born only a few miles apart. Yet, to qualified outside observers such as the Pharisees, they appeared violently alien, hardly born to breathe the same air or serve the same God.

And still, between them stretched an undeniable bond, as if they were halves of one whole, the dark and light of the same truth. They did not walk together, yet it seemed that if you accepted one you must meet and accept the other.

The people sensed that truth without bothering to explain it. The common folk of the streets and fields, who were not gifted with the lofty wisdom and judgment of the Pharisees, slid easily from John to Jesus. The same ones who had let the Baptist wash them in the river now accepted Jesus as their Master, as if it were the most logical move in the world.

The Pharisees put it down to the fanatic tenor of the times. The people, they said, were hungry for religion of any kind. They would follow anyone who talked of God, though how the same men could be disciples of both John and Jesus was more than they could see!

John set himself up as a prophet in the old tradition. He loomed in the desert with all the fire of a new Elias. He was a whirlwind, hurling himself against sloth and evil, pounding at men's hearts to open and do penance.

His food was winged locusts, wild honey, and tree gum, his clothes of rough camel's hair. Self-discipline, silence, and fasting honed the blade of his zeal. And he burst on the world with the taut call of a heart aching for redemption, like a crescendo of all the echoes of the past:

"Repent! The kingdom of God is at hand!"

He was even born, so men said, the way prophets should be born—the prayers of an old childless couple had been answered by an angel.

And, like other prophets before him, John feared no one. So now John was in prison, in the foul cellars of Herod's palace east of the Dead Sea. Like Jezebel before her, Queen Herodias did not like holy men who called her names she deserved. . . .

The people had thought John might be the Christ. But John made it clear he was not.

He had come to prepare the way for Him, to be His messenger crying in the wilderness. He had baptized men with water as a sign of repentance, and begged them to make ready for the Christ. And John had stretched a bony finger through the dank Jordan air to point to the One.

The One He pointed to was Jesus of Nazareth—a Man in ordinary clothes, eating ordinary food, a Carpenter Whom no one in the world could confuse with an ancient prophet.

John had said the Christ would baptize with the Holy Ghost and with fire. He had said the Christ would gather the wheat into barns and burn the chaff with unquenchable fire. The ax was to be laid to the root of the trees. . . .

And here in the market place stood Jesus of Nazareth without fire or ax.

It seemed, to the Pharisees, ridiculous. Compared to John, Jesus was like a spring morning after a night of storm, mild, joyous, a complete anticlimax.

Even the Pharisees had in a way been proud of John's eccentricities. They felt, quite rightly, that only in Israel could such a man be found. It was just that his zeal was excessive.

But Jesus of Nazareth did not belong in the picturesque tradition of prophets. For a would-be Messiah, His behavior was scandalous.

Yet the people who had followed John's austerity now clustered happily around Jesus, and they did not seem to find the contrast ridiculous at all. Two or three of His twelve disciples had been sent to Him by John in the first place. And His miracles had convinced thousands of others. Only last week Jesus had raised a thoroughly dead young man out of his coffin in the middle of his own funeral procession!

It had happened at Naim, not eight miles from Jesus' home town of Nazareth. With one word Jesus had brought a widow's only son back to life. John the Baptist had never done such a thing. Who had ever raised someone from the dead? Elias had, at Sunam, which was, come to think of it, quite near Naim. But Elias had sweated and prayed and groaned and worked for hours. Jesus of Nazareth had simply spoken, and life and death obeyed.

That was enough for the people. To the Pharisees it was only another riddle to ponder.

Far to the south in his dungeon John heard of that miracle and exulted. He sent two of his disciples to Jesus, that they might hear from His own lips the truth, the admission that He was the Messiah.

They came to Him, gaunt men of the desert, in the town market. They found Him in the center of a crowd of people, while the Pharisees stood carefully apart.

"Are You the One Who is to come? Or do we look for another?"

The crowd stretched grizzled necks to look at the fire-eyed strangers. The ambassadors of the Baptist faced the Son of Man, and it was like a muted collision of worlds.

Jesus bowed gravely to them. And then He did a strange

thing. Without a word He began to walk through the thick throng of the bazaar, stopping first at one unknown and then another.

It was an hour such as the world had never known, one hour of wonder poured upon wonder. He touched an old woman, and her blind eyes saw. A lame boy leaped to his feet. Festering wounds healed to new skin while men blinked an eye. Deaf ears opened. Tumors and growths vanished as He bent over them.

He said nothing. But the crowd, wheeling and turning and pressing after Him, whispered and chattered and gabbled, breaking into hoarse shouts of acclaim, wrenched apart with gladness and astonishment, overcome with the glory of that hour.

At last He came again to the center of the square. And He said to the two strangers: "Go and tell John what you have heard and seen. The blind see. The lame walk. The lepers are made clean. The deaf hear. The dead rise again. And to the poor the gospel is preached."

Then suddenly He smiled and said: "And blessed is he whoever shall not be scandalized in Me!"

John's messengers understood. The gospel, the good news, was here. The Light of the World had come. The world might not comprehend the Light, but He had come. It was for this that John lay in the darkness, for this that all the prophets had walked the earth.

The messengers of John were not scandalized. The people were not scandalized. They who had trudged to the Jordan to hear John and do penance were not surprised by joy. Though they could not have put it in words, they understood that they walked now a bridge between the old and the new —that it was as if from the pain of the past the future was even now being born.

But the Pharisees did not understand. And they were scandalized.

When Jesus spoke again it was of them.

Around Him rustled the smiles and tears of men and women still locked in the impact of miracles. Here and there mothers clung to their children, husbands and wives locked hands, trembling with the sudden gift of health. And beyond that circle, perched in neat caution, aloof from emotions, sat the Pharisees, pale and expressionless, watching in silence.

"To what shall I compare the men of this generation? What are they like?" That sad patient smile leaped like a challenge over the heads of the crowd.

"They are like children sitting in the market place, and speaking to one another, and saying: 'We have piped to you and you have not danced! We have mourned, and you have not wept!'"

The throng near Jesus cocked their heads, half puzzled, half amused. Everyone knew the exasperating stubbornness of children who refuse to play—the ones who want to be coaxed, and then delight in sitting back and passing judgment on their friends. They will not be merry. They will not be sad. They sit hugging their loneliness to them like a cloak filched from their parents' wardrobe, looking for ways to convince the world that they are not children at all!

A man, not far from Jesus, said under his breath that when his children acted like that he shook them till they forgot there were such things as moods and tantrums.

A woman, mother of nine, snorted. The only thing to do with such children, she said, was to ignore them.

But what did spoiled children have to do with this generation of Pharisees? What kind of parable was this? The Pharisees raised polite eyebrows. The people waited.

And then Jesus made His meaning clear beyond all question.

He fixed His eyes on the Pharisees and He said:

"John the Baptist came neither eating bread nor drinking wine, and you say: 'He has a devil!'

"The Son of Man has come eating and drinking, and you say: 'Behold a man that is a glutton and a drinker of wine!'"

For that instant His voice, usually so firm and clear, was twisted with all the petulance and disdain of His enemies, a mimicry devastatingly accurate.

And from the crowd laughter rose like a sudden cloud to surround the Pharisees. He had used the parable deftly as a dagger, pinning them to the wall with truth.

What would please them? Not the prophets, not the Christ —not repentance or joy, not expectation or fulfillment. They were like children sulking in a corner, unchildlike, proud, half dead to the call of life.

There is a time for weeping and a time for laughter—and both are parts of life. They walk hand in hand, and if you follow one you cannot help but meet the other. Yet there are those who will not yield to any call, those too sullen to be stirred—the Pharisees of then and now.

Only a childlike heart is wise enough to weep and to dance in season, young enough to feel both winter and spring, to quicken to the rhythm of dark and dawn. The children who will not play, the children who wear the mask of judgment, will be left sitting in the market place alone.

"Wisdom," He said, "will be justified by *all* her children."

Jesus smiled. Through the crowd the two disciples of John made their way, carrying with them the treasure and the light of joy they had found.

And the Pharisees, arms folded, sucked their cheeks, as if testing the bitter taste of scandal.

He turned and left them there in the market place to find their own way home.

21

THE BARREN FIG TREE [*]

HE LIVED in a world all His own, where current events had no more meaning than clouds in the sky.

News in Israel traveled by mouth, from peddler to buyer, from begger to almsgiver, from woman to woman at the well. The market place became a bank in which men deposited rumor and fact, drawing it out with interest. There one could find the latest word on the emperor's court in Rome, hushed horror tales of executions, reports on Pilate's intrigues. Herod Antipas was said to be planning a small war against the king of Arabia Petraea, whose daughter he had pushed aside to marry his own brother's wife, the rasp-eyed, red-lipped Herodias. The water supply in Jerusalem was running low again. The Romans had imported actors from the capital for the new theater. The barley crop was thin this year. Prices were going up. A new tax was planned. A man died, beaten by bandits, on the road to Jericho. . . .

It was important to keep in touch with the world. Men thrived on the urgent color of the talk of the bazaars. Over a rare drink of Egyptian beer, perhaps, or a cup of wine, minds felt more alert, part of the main stream of history even here in the provincial backwaters. Life seemed a little more real,

[*] Luke 13:1–9.

more dramatic, while the threads of the whole world passed through your fingers to be weighed and judged for meaning.

Yet Jesus of Nazareth never listened. He had no time for the things of the hour. And, though He did not forbid His Twelve to go to the market and hear the talk, He kept them so busy that for weeks at a time they would be isolated from all news, living as if in an eggshell.

They could see why He was not interested in palace gossip and spicy tales. But they felt forlorn, ignoring the whole pageant of news. They were homesick for word of Galilee. And they felt it only prudent to know what went on in the Temple, to forearm themselves against the schemes of the Pharisees.

When they could, the Twelve used their ears. And at night, as they sat talking, they speculated on the import of things that happened in the cities, searching for a pattern in the jumble of events. They had come lately to see the fine hand of heaven in every calamity. When a Pharisee dropped dead in the sunshine they felt they knew why. A tax collector's home was destroyed by sudden storm, the Romans in their fancy villas in Capharnaum were stricken to their beds after a dinner of tainted pork. . . .

Then came startling news from Galilee, brought by men who cornered Jesus outside the little synagogue, blurting out the latest reports about the Roman governor—Pontius Pilate.

The people of Palestine hated Pilate—a compliment he heartily returned. The last governor before him had worked hard to ease the friction between Rome and the Jews. But Pilate loathed the Jews. He delighted in insulting them.

Rome intended for the Jews to keep their religion, to run their own Temple without interference or harm. Pilate began his rule by insisting that the robes and vestments of the high priests must be kept in *his* castle. When the Jews wanted to hold a service, let them come and beg Pilate for the use of their ceremonial garments. It was not a move calculated to endear the governor to pious Jews.

Rome knew that Jews believed it a sin to make an image of anything under the sun or beyond. So Rome suggested to her men in Palestine that the standards of the Empire be displayed only when necessary, and then with tact and discretion. Pilate flaunted the eagle-topped standards, the giant banners with the picture of the emperor-god, all over the holy city of Jerusalem. He dangled them from his castle, on the side facing directly toward the Temple. Only an appeal to the emperor himself forced Pilate to remove those flags.

These facts men and women all over Israel knew. Each fresh outrage of Pilate sped on the air from Jerusalem till even the salt sellers of villages in the plains knew it before dawn.

But the news the men of Galilee brought was more shocking yet.

Pilate had decided Jerusalem needed a better water supply. Being a Roman, he intended to build an aqueduct, this one to reach from the Pools of Solomon up near Bethlehem through the hills to the city. It would be a tremendous engineering feat. It would also be expensive. Pilate's treasury was low. So Pilate took the money he needed from the sacred treasuries of the Jewish Temple. That was money offered to God in sacrifices by the holy people of Israel, money of their own minting, designed only for the service of heaven. It was sacrilege.

The men from Galilee, their robes still stained with the sweat and dust of their journey, paused to gauge the effect of their news.

Jesus nodded gravely, as if He were not at all surprised, and said nothing.

"Then—then some of our own men of Galilee were killed,

butchered by Pilate till their own blood ran and coated their sacrifice money in the streets!"

"And, Master, those who died were men who heard You and did not heed You. One I knew well, and he even ate the bread and fish with You that day on the other side of the lake, and he went home and went right on living with his same sins."

"Another one that *I* knew never gave a penny to the poor. A meaner man never lived—or died!"

The Twelve pressed around the news bearers, their faces solemn. Lightning had struck close to home, the vengeance of God on those who deserved it, perhaps. They looked at Jesus, waiting now for Him to confirm the meaning of the news.

Jesus sighed. "Do you think that those Galileans were sinners worse than all other men of Galilee, because they suffered such things? No, I say to you—but unless you do penance you shall all perish too."

His eyes rested sadly on their flushed cheeks.

"Or those eighteen on whom the tower fell in Siloe and killed them—do you think they also were debtors, more than all the men that lived in Jerusalem?"

The Twelve blinked. They had not known He had even heard of that tragedy. But Jesus continued:

"No, I say to you—but except you do penance, you shall all likewise perish."

The men of Galilee looked at each other. They felt suddenly as if all the air had gone out of them. They became aware that in their hurry to tell the tale to Jesus they had not yet found lodging, nor eaten since their overnight camp by the river.

The disciples were embarrassed. Peter looked as if he wanted to get out of the sun. Andrew, who knew these men of Galilee personally, seemed to want to apologize to them, but he could think of nothing to say.

Then Jesus spoke again, and His voice was like a cool breeze driving away the dust and clouds of misunderstanding. He leaned back on his elbows against the vine-covered wall of the synagogue garden and told them the tale of the barren fig tree.

"A certain man," He said, "had a fig tree planted in his vineyard. And he came looking for fruit on it and found none.

"And he said to the vinedresser: 'Look, for more than three years I have come seeking for fruit on this fig tree, and I find none. Cut it down therefore! Why let it cumber the ground?'"

The men listening found it a most reasonable command. Fig trees did not grow thickly, after all. Only in a few towns could you find groves of them. A man had one fig tree in his yard, no more. And if that tree did not behave and yield fruit, why give it room? Three years was plenty of time to judge.

Jesus continued: "But the vinedresser, answering, said to him: 'Lord, let it alone this year also, while I dig around it and manure it. And see if it bears fruit. But if not, then after that you shall cut it down!'"

A fig tree is meant to bear fruit. Its leaves are broad and green, but it is not designed for shade or for beauty. It cannot simply stand in the yard and preen itself in the sunlight. If it does not respond to the loving hopeful care of the gardener it is no better than a weed or a thornbush.

That much they could see. But His eyes left no doubt that this parable was about them—about all men granted reprieve, another day of life in which to bear fruit. And what fruit were they to produce?

Unless you do penance you too shall perish.

His words whispered in their hearts, and they understood.

They had thought the slaughter by Pilate, the seemingly chance fall of a tower, a judgment on others—and he was warning them of their own judgment.

They had told him of Pilate's outrages, half hoping He would rise in wrath to condemn pagan offenses against Israel. And He had not condemned them. He had taken them for granted, as part of the pattern of life—old, not new.

It was true that even then the signs of disaster were in the air, advance warnings of the day when Rome would destroy Jerusalem. But that day outside the synagogue Jesus spoke to men of all time and all nations. His parable was not hobbled by current events.

Towers still fall. Governments still persecute. The news has not changed much in two thousand years. Nor have the habits of fig trees and gardeners, of men and of God.

Jesus had come to stir all souls to new life, to feed and tend them with the sharp edge of truth. And the soul that does not respond to His care and bring forth fruit for Him will be cut down. The time of ransom is short. It was running out then for the men of Galilee, for the Twelve, as it is now for all who still hear the homely tale of the fig tree with no figs.

It was a very small parable, the kind that could go unnoticed in the clamor of the day, then as now.

Jesus thanked the men of Galilee most courteously for coming to Him and made His way through the market place to the small house where He stayed. A caravan had just come to town, rich in the heady perfume of doings in far-off places, in palaces and alleys. He passed through it unaware.

He did live in a world of His own, the world of that good news which men today call the gospel.

22

THE TWO DEBTORS*

THERE was, men felt, a flame in Him that leaped like altar fire, raising everything it touched to new heights.

It was as if He were almost torn apart by tenderness, as if it took heroic strength to contain His own heart.

It seemed only love that kept Him alive.

Children tugged at His tunic and women sang after He passed. Men who had looked into those overwhelming eyes turned back to the day's work with new serenity.

"God is love," He said. And those words sent tremors of disturbance into the cold recesses of the Temple and caught the people of the streets by surprise.

Of course, everyone knew you were commanded to love God. But it was hard to say exactly what that meant. Certainly there was no room for emotionalism in the Temple. Certainly too, in spite of certain passages in Scripture, it seemed obvious that human love was a thing completely apart from God.

Yet Jesus of Nazareth, to the horror of the Pharisees and the gentle astonishment of the people, appeared as much interested in the heart as in the soul. As far as the Pharisees

---

* Luke 7:36–50.

could see, He placed a premium on any kind of love, short of sin.

And even when it came to sin He was unorthodox.

There was that night that He dined at the house of Simon the Pharisee, the night the harlot came.

Jesus had been invited to Simon's, not from friendship but from curiosity. The Pharisees intended to bait and test this prophet from Nazareth. Deliberately they omitted the usual formalities as they received Him as a guest. He made no comment. They presumed He did not know a snub when He met one.

Then suddenly, uninvited, she came. Apparently she knew her way about Simon's house. At least she had no trouble getting past his servants. Bold as ever, she entered the room where Jesus and Simon and his friends reclined on cushions at table. In her hands shone a pale white alabaster box of ointment, a treasure few women could afford. Without a word she knelt at Jesus' feet.

The men at the table propped themselves higher on their elbows to see what would happen.

She was weeping, silently, as if the anguish of her soul were too deep for sound. And with her tears she washed Jesus' feet, more abject than a slave, more tender than a mother caressing her child. Once she raised the large round gray eyes to His face, as if pleading for what she could not say. Then, tears ended, she unwound the coiled knots of her dark hair—the hair she had tended with such pride—and, gathering it in her hands like a cloth, she rubbed his feet dry.

Simon had been unable to speak when he first saw her move through the curtained arch of the room. He had watched in astonishment as she embarked on her strange ritual. But when she turned her hair to a towel he could not be still. A snort shattered the silence and Simon, bending forward, took two pressed fig cakes from a bowl, cocked a wink at his other guests, and began to eat.

The woman dried Jesus' feet, bent, and kissed them. And then, opening the alabaster box, she rubbed the ointment over His ankles and toes. Fragrance filled the room like incense in the Temple. Simon wrinkled his nose and brushed a crumb from his beard.

It just goes to show, he thought to himself, that this Jesus is an impostor and a nobody. If He were a prophet He would know who this woman is and what kind of sinner it is who touches Him. Simon began to savor the way this story would sound when he could tell it in Jerusalem. He was glad there were other guests. Without witnesses, who would believe such a tale?

But Jesus cut through his thoughts as if they were transparent.

"Simon," He said, "I have something to say to you."

Simon smiled and waved a grand hand. *"Master—say it!"*

The woman lay at His feet, her lips still pressed in a kiss. And when Jesus spoke, though He addressed Himself to Simon, it was on her that His eyes rested.

"A certain creditor," said Jesus, "had two debtors." He glanced briefly at Simon, as if for corroboration. Simon nodded.

"One owed him five hundred denarii, and the other fifty," Jesus continued. "And since neither one had the wherewithal to pay—he forgave them both."

The room was so still that the candle flames flickered with His breath.

"Which one of the two," He asked, "do you think loves him most?"

Simon sniffed and reached for a honey cake with almonds. "I suppose the one to whom he forgave the most." And his tone implied that "love" was an oddly strong word to use in a business transaction.

Jesus bent His head. "You have judged rightly."

His gaze reached out from under His heavy brows to the woman on her knees. "Simon," He said, "do you see this woman? I entered your house and you gave Me no water for My feet. But she with her tears has washed My feet and with her hair has wiped them. You gave Me no kiss. But since she came in she has not ceased to kiss My feet. You did not anoint My head with oil, but she with ointment has anointed My feet."

Slowly, gracefully, Jesus stood, till the height of Him dominated the room, casting a shadow over all at table. And to the woman He said:

"Your sins are forgiven you."

As He stretched His hand to rest on her tangled head the guests at table gasped with that half-choked horror that is near laughter: "Who is this that forgives sins also?"

But Jesus spoke only to the woman. "Your faith has made you safe," He said. "Go in peace."

It was, the Pharisees would agree later, an incredible, scandalous scene, an exhibition not soon forgotten. It should be enough to destroy Him in the eyes of all decent men.

It was not forgotten. The parable of the two debtors, and its setting, would be all over town before morning. It would be told and retold to uncounted ears, century after century. But it would not destroy Jesus. It would strike only at those who had not yet learned the secret of love.

The one who owes the most, and is forgiven, loves the most. It was sometimes so in borrowing and lending here on earth, said Matthew as the Twelve pondered the tale. He had seen a man rescued from bankruptcy go wild with thanks. A little debt forgiven means less—sad, but true.

And the same is true of sinners. Matthew knew that he, of all the Twelve, had the greatest cause to love Jesus. The others had been decent folk. He had been a publican. Never would he forget the dizzying grandeur of the Love that called to him: "Follow Me!"

The woman had been a public sinner. And she had been converted from sin. Some said it was the preaching of John the Baptist that had struck her first, almost a year before. Whatever it was, she had wakened to the enormous love of God. The gift of forgiveness, the treasure of divine tenderness, was hers. And she had done what she could to express a love that would not be contained.

It is, thought Matthew, a love that belongs to all of us. We are all debtors who cannot pay, rescued by majestic forgiveness of God. And there is not one who can claim his debt is small, not one who could have earned his own way to freedom. Only the love of God redeems us. And that love is the greatest gift He gives, greater even than the release from debt. For in love is life. . . .

In all the years to come men would find endless mystery in the evening at Simon's house. Was it because of her love that she was forgiven? Or did her faith win forgiveness, and forgiveness beget love? Could you say that the same greatness of heart that led to sin drove her on to the transforming love of God? It was a riddle only He could answer.

But this much was plain. Forgiven, she loved Christ with her whole heart, her whole mind, and her whole strength—surrendering pride and vanity and human respect in the one perfect gift of herself.

And that was the way for all souls to love, the way God Himself loves, beyond reason.

The forgiveness of the world's sin was to come not through

a formal ritual, polite and self-contained—but by a love that shook the world from the Cross.

That scandal still lay in the future the night Jesus left the house of Simon the Pharisee.

The fragrance of the ointment hung heavy over the table. Simon called a servant to air the room and reached for another cake with the comfortable manner of a man who is sure he is in no one's debt.

23

THE GREAT SUPPER*

H<small>E WAS</small> a most difficult guest—interesting, but difficult.

His manners were perfect, which did rather startle them. He was not a wild-eyed uncombed kind of prophet at all. His Galilean accent was not impossibly coarse. And there was about Him an aura of warmth that seemed to spark the air with festivity. Men said His cousin, John the Baptist, had been a sour, joyless individual. This Jesus was not.

The trouble was that He seemed as much at ease here at this table as if He were the host and they the guests.

When He first came to Perea, many strange stories followed Him down from Jerusalem and across the Jordan. And this sabbath day the leading Pharisees of Perea had invited Him to dinner—more as a curiosity to be studied than as a guest of honor.

The event had been planned carefully. The richest of the Pharisees, a man who dealt in both imported dyes and olive oil, prepared a supper and invited his guests well ahead of time. Only the most pious and the most intricately learned minds were to come, a battery of questioners to expose the ignorance of this street preacher.

He was, obviously, a menace to all men of true faith.

* Luke 14:7–24.

The people of the streets, the uneducated, unclean multitudes, hailed Him as a miracle worker, a prophet. Some even called Him the Messiah. The Pharisees of Jerusalem, staunch defenders of the faith, considered Him dangerous—a rebel, a blasphemer, a religious trickster.

And these local Pharisees of Perea, who considered themselves competent authorities on religion, would decide for themselves. They invited Him to dine.

He accepted their invitation pleasantly enough. He greeted the other guests courteously, parrying their questions with a smile. His learning surprised them. His conduct disarmed them.

And then, quite calmly, He had worked a miracle before them, right in the reception room. A man with dropsy had come in and pushed his way to Jesus. And in the midst of a discussion over the technicalities of what was permitted on the sabbath in the way of work, Jesus had cured the stranger —on the sabbath.

Such behavior made conversation awkward, to say the least.

He had gone in to dinner with the Pharisees, and while they discussed who should sit where He had produced two short sermons—one on humility, the other on charity.

That was easier to accept. Prophets always preached. Of course, Jesus chose uncomfortable examples. He had said it was better to take the lowest place at table than the highest. And He had said it was better to entertain the poor than the rich. He was blunt, they decided, but naïve.

They sat then to eat, reclining on cushions beside the low table. And one of them, looking Jesus blandly in the face, said piously:

"Blessed is he who shall eat bread in the kingdom of God!"

And there was in the way he said it the clear smugness

of the Pharisee who fully intended God to reward him with heaven.

Jesus raised His head. And in that movement these men caught a glint of kingliness, and they remembered that in this Carpenter's veins ran the blood of the royal line of David.

And Jesus began then to tell them a story, a parable, the same kind for which He was famous in the streets.

"A certain man planned a great supper and invited many," said Jesus, His eyes brooding over the self-satisfied faces around Him. "And when the time came for the supper he sent his servant to tell those who were invited that they should come, for everything was ready. And they all began to make excuses."

Sadness filtered in His young voice. He looked up into the arched ceiling of the dining hall and continued:

"The first said to him, 'I have bought a farm and I need to go and see it. I pray you, hold me excused.'"

The mimicry of the consummate actor shaped the story now. The guests grinned as characters one by one leaped to life in His voice.

"And another said, 'I have bought five pairs of oxen, and I am on my way to try them out. Please, excuse me.'

"And another said, 'I have married a wife, and so I cannot come.'

"And the servant, returning, told these things to his master and the master was very angry."

The guests turned to smile at their own host. Who would not be angry if the acceptance of a dinner invitation were broken at the last minute, when all was ready?

But His voice commanded their attention, reminding them that this was no idle tale. Had they not been speaking only a moment before of feasting not on earth but in the kingdom of God? He continued:

"Then the master of the house said to his servant: 'Go out quickly into the streets and lanes of the city, and bring in here the poor, the feeble, the blind, and the lame!'"

They watched Him now, weighing His words in the slanting afternoon sunlight.

"And the servant did as he was told, and came back to say: 'Lord, it is done, and still there is room for more.'

"Then the lord said to his servant: 'Go out into the highways and hedges and compel them to come in, so that my house may be filled.

"'But I say to you—not one of those men who were first invited shall taste of my supper!'"

What did it mean, that strange drastic action of the lord of the supper? These Pharisees knew a parable when they heard one, knew and appreciated Jesus' habit of speaking of heaven in terms of earth. Their minds were agile, swift to leap to hidden meanings. For them He did not need to spell out the parallels. The lord of the supper was the Lord of heaven, that they knew.

And there were no fit excuses for postponing the Lord's wishes, that was clear. Buying and selling, marrying and loving, important though they were, must never interfere with the salvation of a soul. A well-mannered man on earth would not let his private affairs intrude on a social obligation. And yet, it was true, men did let business and pleasure shoulder aside the duties of religion at times.

One Pharisee permitted himself an approving smile at the cleverness of the tale. But Jesus, watching him, seemed to press him to further thought.

If you were invited and refused at the last minute you did not get a second chance. If you forfeited the invitation, which was your right to heaven, another would take your place. The poor, the outcasts, would crowd into the feast, for there was to be a supper no matter what riffraff came.

The Pharisee who had spoken first to Jesus of eating bread in the kingdom of God pursed his lips. It seemed unreasonable of the Lord to design heaven for the scourings of the slums, to be so persistent that He would welcome anyone at all to fill up His table! Of course, he thought, the parable was not quite accurate, for most of those who would be called to heaven would not fail to come. Like himself, like all Pharisees, they would be punctilious in meeting God's demands, would they not?

He read the answer in Jesus' dark eyes. The answer was that they would not!

With a gasp these men caught the full meaning of His parable. He had been talking about them.

They, the Pharisees, were the ones first invited by God's messenger. And they had accepted the invitation as their due. But at the last moment, when all was ready, they would meet God's Messenger and turn Him away with excuses—that was the kernel of this parable! This Jesus dared say to their faces that they would not recognize the urgency of the final call to the feast when it came. They would not have another chance.

The Messenger of God would go instead then to the streets and alleys to call the poor and the humble, the ones not so skilled in the law, not so professional in their religion. And the scorned and outcast would obey the invitation of the Lord's servant. And they would enter the house of the Lord.

That was what Jesus had meant by His tale of the great supper.

Within a few years the world would see still another meaning in the parable. Men would see that the Jews as a whole were those first invited, and that as a group they would reject the call. And God would welcome the Gentiles into His house instead.

If He came to our dinner table today, would He tell us the same story? The heart of the parable lives for all time. There are modern Pharisees, in tweed jackets instead of embroidered robes. And He might well fix His gaze on those whom God has called into Christianity, who are entitled to enter heaven and who still make fatal excuses.

The Christian today might be more interested in a new expansion in business, a chance to make a quick profit, than in a farm. Some might not want five yoke of oxen, but they might put a new automobile, a television set, a fresh interior decoration job before obedience to God's will. And are there not Christians today who care more for the love of a man and woman than the love of God?

To answer His invitation we have to be willing to leave all things and come instantly. It is as simple, and as difficult, as that.

And we must listen to His servant when He brings us word.

If He came tonight, could He not find the need to tell such a parable to us?

The dinner was over. It broke up in silence.

And Jesus, the guest, rose from the table and left. The Messenger of God walked out of the house of the Pharisees, into the streets and lanes of the city, into the highways and hedgerows—carrying the word of the Lord.

24

THE BUILDING OF A TOWER*

H<small>E DID</small> not seem to want to make His a popular movement, at all.

It did not make sense to the Twelve. Whoever heard of a
Master who did not rejoice with every new face following in
His wake? How could you establish a kingdom of any kind,
even of heaven, if you did not welcome any and every new
adherent?

But there were times when Jesus seemed to go out of His
way to discourage people and send them home.

This particular morning in the province of Perea, for instance, half the town was out. A stranger would have thought
there was a holiday parade, the way people trooped down
the streets, through the bazaars, and out into the hills east
of Jordan.

The Twelve were on top of the world. The sunlit air seemed
to crackle with adventure and hilarity. Half a thousand souls
were hurrying to keep up with the swift stride of Jesus, a
small army clamoring and laughing with the heady excitement of following Him.

Yet from the look on His face you might think He was ac-

* Luke 14:25–30.

tually impatient with them. He did not turn His head, did not even raise His hand in greeting.

He had worked two impressive miracles for the people of Perea, two cures that had spread a brush fire of enthusiasm.

On the sabbath He had gone to the synagogue to teach. And while He was teaching He had seen a pitifully grotesque figure in the back on the women's side of the room—a cripple literally bent double, her head so far down that she could not lift her eyes to see. Eighteen years she had been this way, crooked as a hairpin.

Jesus laid His hands on her and instantly she stood upright, the blood draining from her head, and a burst of joy on her lips.

The head of the synagogue had denounced Jesus for healing on the sabbath when no work was permitted. But the people had gone wild with praise for this miracle-working teacher come from God.

Later, on the same day, while dining with His enemies the Pharisees, Jesus had healed a man all swollen and puffed with dropsy. And the news of that cure flared like sunset glare through every door and window in the town.

That was why the people followed Him now. They had heard Him preach of the kingdom of heaven. They had witnessed His miraculous power. And their fervor had driven them after Him.

"What else did He expect?" whispered one of the Twelve. "If He did not want them to come and follow Him why did He bother to draw attention to Himself?"

"He looks as if He does not care whether they come or not. But surely He does not want just twelve as disciples and no more? What kind of kingdom is twelve men?"

They walked with the jovial crowds at their backs and the

grave-faced Jesus ahead of them. And to tell the truth, the Twelve were a bit exasperated with Him.

Like a few religious experts today, they wanted to do a super-selling job on the kingdom of heaven, and clinch the deal before enthusiasm had time to cool. Get the people into the movement, then educate them afterward. Catch them on the crest of emotion, they felt, before they give up and go home and forget about Christ.

That was, after all, the way of all leaders and of all salesmen in the world.

"For their sake, if not for His own, wouldn't it be better for them to be encouraged in this mood? It is almost cruel of Him to pay so little attention to what is really a wonderful demonstration!"

Just then Jesus stopped on the grassed top of a small hill and turned to face the crowds. Those nearest Him stopped too, and those behind clustered close, peering on tiptoe over the shoulders of those ahead. The hubbub and laughter faded. The last stragglers found rocks for perches. It was suddenly very quiet in the Perean hills.

Then Jesus' voice rang through the air like a challenge. He spoke slowly, distinctly, that no breeze should steal His words.

"If any man follow Me," He said, "and does not hate his father and mother and wife and children and brethren, yes, and even his own life—he cannot be My disciple."

Hate? They had all heard Him use that word this way before. They knew what He meant. Not that a man must break the law of God by hating anyone—enemy or parent. But that a man must not love these more than God.

He was saying simply that to be His disciple a man must place service and love of God before anything else, before the demands of family or of self, before even his own life. He

must be willing to renounce them as completely as if he did
hate them, if it became necessary for the love of God. If a
mother or father ordered a man to do what God would not
want him to do, he must serve the greater Love and obey the
greater Law. A wife's tears or pleading must never win a man
to sin. To follow Christ a man must be willing to sacrifice his
own life.

He flung those words at those lighthearted crowds as if
daring them to follow Him at such a price.

And many there remembered the parable He had told
them of the great supper, when those invited refused to come
because they had just married a wife or bought a farm. . . .

"And anyone who does not carry his cross and come after
Me," cried Jesus now, "cannot be My disciple!"

Carry a cross? Who could understand that? Only the worst
of condemned criminals carried a cross, the gibbet on which
they would be nailed to die. It was genuine torture to carry
that heavy crossbeam. Your hands were tied to it and you
struggled in misery to balance and walk. Could it be that
hard to follow Christ?

The crowds looked at each other and murmured. Here and
there men started to edge their way to the rear, ready to leave
this madman, miracle worker and prophet though He might
be.

The Twelve stared up at Jesus, wondering.

And He spoke then in a parable, a warning for all spur-of-
the-moment Christians of all time.

"Which of you," He said, "having in mind to build a tower,
does not first sit down and calculate the cost involved, to see
whether you will have the wherewithal to finish it?"

And a small smile, wonderfully gentle, touched His cheeks.
"Otherwise," He said, "after he has laid the foundation and

then is not able to finish it, everyone who sees it will begin to mock him!"

In spite of themselves, the people grinned. Then, as now, the world was full of men who leaped before they looked, and launched great projects without counting the cost. There was the man who set out to have the biggest farm of barley and could not even finish plowing a tenth of it before the time for seeding came. And the man who boasted he was going to send all his sons to study in Jerusalem under the great rabbis, till he learned the price of it. His sons were still at home. There were then and now children who planned building giant castles of rock and quit before they had half a wall built. And men who were like children, fired with world-shaking enthusiasm one day—a sparkless laughing-stock the next.

Count the cost first, men said. Be sure you know what you are doing. Don't run off half cocked. Only fools rush in without thinking.

And that was precisely what Jesus was saying.

The Twelve, watching Him, remembered their own call. They had indeed left everything to follow Him. But He had not accepted them fully as disciples till several months later, till He had let them know clearly what they were undertaking. Their lives, they knew, were at stake with Him. And they realized that He had never underplayed the danger. A disciple who had to be lured was not a disciple.

Nor is the decision to follow Christ a light one. It involves more than marriage, more than life or death, more than building the world's greatest tower. It must not be made in a frenzy of a moment. It must be weighed by each soul individually, with sober thought.

Jesus knew why the Pereans had come trooping after Him.

He had become an overnight sensation. He had caught the public fancy.

But Jesus Christ is not a sensation. He does not deal in passing enthusiasms. The service of Christ is a lifelong work, more demanding, more noble than any other human action. The eternal God does not rest His claims on mob reaction or on the day's shining glory of a miracle.

It would, Jesus was saying, be better not to come at all than to come and then find the price beyond you. At least it is more honest to face the cross and refuse it than to quit when it falls on your shoulders.

He most definitely did not want what men call a "popular movement." He came not to sway a crowd or pack heaven with freeloaders. He came to call a soul in intimate love and surrender, to remold it into the image of Himself. He came to save the whole world. But He would save it one by one, soul by soul. And He would save each soul not for an hour, not for a month of high fervor, but for eternity.

He would not pretend it was easy. He would not conceal the cost. Not if the whole world refused Him and left.

He was, after all, the soul of honesty, the God of truth.

And the tower His followers would build would lead to heaven.

25

THE LOST SHEEP°

H E   W A S at home in all parts of human life—at wedding
or funeral, at rich men's dinners and poor women's kitchens.
He was a carpenter, they knew, but like a boy who watches
his elders and remembers every detail, this Jesus seemed to
have caught the rhythm and pattern of a hundred different
careers. He knew the ways of pearl traders in the bazaars, of
stewards of vast estates, and of kings. But above all He knew
and loved the habits of the men of the fields.

Shepherds He loved with special affection. The herders of
Bethlehem had been the first to hear the news of His birth,
the first outside His family to kneel before Him. Since the
time of David, His ancestor, the man tending the flocks had
been for the Jews a symbol of God watching over His people.

The odd thing is that by the time Christ came on the scene
shepherds in general had become religious outcasts!

The Pharisees, who were the recognized authorities on
such matters, considered shepherds quite beyond the pale.
Because of their work they were unable to attend to all the
tiny details of worship as prescribed by the thousand laws of
Pharisaical tradition. Shepherds could not always go to the
Temple to offer sacrifice at the proper time. They were not

° Matthew 18:12–14; Luke 15:1–7.

likely to observe the sabbath properly out on the mountain-sides, nor keep the other vigils and feasts, nor submit to ritual cleansing.

So the shepherds were under rabbinical ban, part of the great "cursed multitude" who could not possibly contrive to please God or go to heaven. It was a bit as if our best Christians condemned telephone operators and doctors and nurses because they had to work on Sundays.

The fact that Abraham and Moses and David were all shepherds seemed not to impress the Pharisees at all!

But, on the other hand, the Pharisees did not impress Jesus either.

They were heckling Him again this particular day in Perea, niggling at Him on the same old score—the fact that He was not a spiritual snob.

They put their hands over their mouths and whispered in loud righteous indignation: "This man welcomes sinners—and what's more, He even dines with them!"

Now, of course, to eat a meal with someone was a sign of friendship of one sort or another in those days as now. And to eat with someone who was unclean with sin was quite as impossible as to eat with a disease carrier or a fisherman who had not bathed. It was not done—at least not when the sin was public knowledge and committed by someone of the spiritual lower classes. Of course, a Pharisee's sins were of a different sort, and could be overlooked by another Pharisee.

It is not so very different now. There are many proper Christians who would not dream of having dinner with girls arrested for soliciting, or with men under sentence for robbery, but who would and do dine with ladies who carry on discreet affairs, or gentlemen who juggle business funds. Sin is less repulsive when accomplished with good manners.

Jesus heard what the Pharisees said. He heard, too, the

rustle of reaction in the crowd that listened, some beginning to doubt His sincerity, some turning their backs on His enemies.

A smile twitched the corners of His lips above the simple short brown beard. He could have told them that, if He were unclean because He ate with sinners, the Pharisees were also defiled because they had eaten with Him! Only two days had passed since these same Pharisees had invited Jesus to dinner —and regretted it. He could have suggested that perhaps they were the sinners with whom He had been accused of dining!

But it is not by trading insults that souls are won. Love and truth are the twin weapons to capture a soul. And Christ, Who loved as no one else has ever loved, knew that He must somehow show the world the truth about the way God looks at sinners.

People then had the idea, quite carefully encouraged by the Pharisees, that there was no hope for the ordinary plain soul, much less for real sinners. God was a kind of cantankerous old man with a thousand rules and an unholy delight in catching people breaking one of them. He was a God with His nose in the air—an overgrown Pharisee.

It was quite a silly idea. It still is. Even today there are people with so little understanding of God that they consider their own cases hopeless from the start. And since they don't see how they can ever be good enough for heaven they quit trying and head the other way.

This, perhaps more than any other thought, Jesus wanted to contradict once and forever.

He stood in the square near the bazaar and faced the Pharisees and the sinners who knew they were sinners as well. His stance, the height of Him with His outspread hands, was like an admission of all the charges made against Him. He bowed

His head solemnly, agreeing with the murmur. He did indeed associate with sinners.

And like a man defending himself in court, He told them then the parable of the Lost Sheep.

"Which man of you," He began, "if he had a hundred sheep and then lost one, would not leave the ninety-nine in the desert and go after the one that is lost until he found it?"

The Pharisees snickered behind their hands. Another shepherd story! As if there were anything to be learned from shepherds! And besides, who would leave ninety-nine to search for one? The percentage was quite beyond common sense. Ninety-nine sheep in the flock were worth more than one lost in the ravine any day.

"And when he has found the sheep, he will lay it on his shoulders rejoicing," said Jesus. And it seemed as if the crowd could see His broad shoulders bend a little with the warm weight of the strayed sheep. It was, they knew, a burden no matter how tamely the sheep rested. But the simple folk of Perea had seen shepherds lugging sheep home on their shoulders even if the Pharisees had not. They knew it was a burden made easy by duty and devotion.

That was one thing about shepherds, the people said. They spent their lives for their sheep with a kind of loyal affection that was far more urgent than the protection of property. A farmer might sit up nights to protect a crop from marauders, or a merchant sacrifice time and money to protect his interests. But a shepherd loved his beasts far more than the price of wool could warrant!

Jesus nodded. "And when he comes home he will call together his friends and neighbors and say: 'Rejoice with me, for I have found my sheep that was lost.'"

The Pharisees looked properly bored.

Jesus continued: "I say to you that in the same way there will be joy in heaven over one sinner who does penance—more than for the ninety-nine just souls who do not need penance!"

The Pharisees gasped. They had been caught unaware. And they found themselves faced now with one of the most daring statements this Jesus had made. He was saying, in effect, that He was the Shepherd and the sinners were His own lost sheep. When He reclaimed them heaven would rejoice, and so He could afford to leave the good to tend themselves while He hunted down the strays.

And if He called Himself the Shepherd He was as good as calling Himself God.

Again and again Isaias the prophet had spoken of God as the shepherd. "He shall gather together the lambs with His arm, and He shall take them up in His bosom, and He Himself shall carry the ones that are with young," said Isaias. "He shall tend His flock like the shepherd."

It was an audacious parable. It also contradicted everything the Pharisees preferred to believe about God.

How could there be more joy over a repentant sinner than over the ones who had always been good? That put a premium on breaking the Law! The way to God's heart was obviously to be wicked till your deathbed and then repent—a bit risky perhaps, but most dramatic. . . .

The Pharisees were scandalized, as anyone would be with such an interpretation. What could you expect, they asked, of a crazy street preacher like this one?

The Pharisees did not understand Him. But the people did. They saw the love in His eyes, and they knew that they were truly His. They understood that the ninety-nine, if they were indeed good, would not mind if the Lord made a fuss over a lost sheep that was found. They would share His joy, for they would share His love, being one with Him.

And they, who knew their own need for rescue by the Shepherd, felt their hearts leap with the understanding that God is all-merciful, the most lovable of beings, the tender Source of Love.

For them the parable of sheep struck into the weave of everyday life. There are few shepherds left in our lives. We do not know first hand the aching search for one of a flock. But the truth of the parable is not gone. We can find our own translations of it.

We can think of a mother and father with nine children, perhaps. And one of those children, through disobedient carelessness, has nearly died from an accident. Those parents would rejoice over that child more than over all the eight who are healthy and wise and cautious and obedient. One nearly died! One was nearly lost—and he is safe again in their arms! And the eight brothers and sisters do not resent the joy their parents show. They share it. They do not expect an extra reward for not having been in peril of death!

Our God loves us more than mother or father, tends us with fiercer devotion than any shepherd. He is the burning heart to which we all belong.

There are Pharisees today to scare us. The world is full of ridiculous ideas of holiness, impossible for us to achieve. But they are not God's own ideas of holiness. He asks only that we trust Him as gently as a lost sheep, and come when He goes in search of us.

He asks us to believe in His love.

26

THE LOST COIN*

It seemed that every soul who spoke to Him was precious in His eyes.

For the sloppiest old woman begging a word of counsel, for tip-nosed young upstarts, for Pharisees and for publicans, young mothers, farm hands, even for children, He had time. He was never too busy. Some men, while they nod and listen, still make you feel they are looking over your shoulder at the next in line, impatient to be rid of your petty troubles. But Jesus looked into your eyes as if He found there the focus of a long search.

There were some who called that good technique, a subtle flattery. Judas said that was what it was. He practiced it on his own, without much success. It was, he found, extraordinarily difficult to pretend interest in someone whose own mother would have found him dull. The world was full of clods and idiots, of snobs and beggars. What could you gain from one of them?

Judas was a practical man, with an eye to the purse. To a possible benefactor he could give undivided attention. He had learned that the most unlikely-looking prospects, the threadbare and lean-looking poor, were actually more apt to

* Luke 15:8–10.

give to the Twelve than the rich. He could spot an open hand
ten feet off. What bothered Judas was that the Master did
not seem able to tell the difference between an active pros-
pect and a dead one—or even to care. From a practical point
of view, His unselective attack was a waste of time. And someone had to use common sense. No kingdom was ever won on
credit.

That was where Judas would be indispensable.

The other eleven had accused Judas of being a money-
grubber. They implied that he sometimes confused his own
purse with the common one, to his advantage. Coming from
someone like Matthew, such a remark was understandable.
Judas himself had thought it odd that Jesus did not ask
Matthew to handle the finances of the group.

The reason, of course, was that even Jesus understood the
value of money, and the other eleven were in no condition to
manage the purse. They were so bedazzled by His teaching
that they were ready to live on air, like wild flowers—a comparison which Judas thought extremely inept for a bunch of
gangly, weedy-bearded disciples. Matthew, since his call by
Jesus, had swung so far away from his old outlook that he
was positively extravagant and irresponsible. He couldn't be
trusted with a penny. He didn't even want a penny!

It was Jesus Who understood that the poor need more than
the gospel, Jesus Who ordered that alms be given discreetly
to those crucified by taxes and the expenses of illness. In that,
at least, He was reasonable. The difficulty was, as far as Judas
could see, that Jesus simply forgot that He and the Twelve
were also poor, and in need of charity.

That was why, when people pressed contributions into
Judas' hands, he began to put only part in the treasury. The
rest he would hoard prudently, as a surprise against the
needs of the new kingdom. If he borrowed from that secret

cache now and then, it was with the express intention of paying it back. . . .

He was only protecting Jesus against Himself. It was a fine
feeling to know that if it were not for him the famous Son
of Man would be at the mercy of the world, the hunger of
the belly, and the tax men. The day would come, surely,
when the revolution dawned, when Jesus the Savior would
lead His precious rabble against the decadent rule of Rome.
That was the Messiah's business on earth. And who would
pay the way to success? Judas smiled. If it were not for
him . . .

In the meantime he was patient with the foibles of His
Master, more tolerant far than the Pharisees. Judas had seen
them cock crooked eyebrows at Jesus in disdain as He
went His way among the great unwashed multitudes. They
thought He defiled Himself in the eyes of God because He
touched those not ritually purified.

Even the rest of the Twelve, for all their devotion to Jesus,
grew uneasy at times. Peter was a proper Jew, to whom the
laws of diet and avoidance of Gentiles were supremely important. Jude and James, who were related to Jesus by blood,
were the same kind. They did not quite understand why He
healed the servant of a Roman centurion, even one coming
highly recommended by men of the synagogue. They had
been miserable that time in Samaria when He had insisted on
talking to the woman at the well, and then to a whole townful
of Samaritans.

They did not understand why He bothered.

If they had asked Judas he would have explained that in
a well-ordered campaign a strategist overlooks no chances.
Every contact was important. Every name was to be remembered. A Roman soldier might prove most helpful. The north-
ern Samaritans, even though they were outsiders, had voices

and strength to give to a cause. As for sinners? Who knew better than they the secrets of the world, the back doors and alleyways of power?

Let others call Jesus a blind idealist. As far as Judas was concerned there was strategy in His madness. He might not know what He was doing. But Judas thought he did, and Judas approved. The personal touch was the key to success.

It was to come as a violent surprise when he realized how completely he had misunderstood Jesus. The shock was enough to unhinge a man. . . .

He should have known that day in Perea, when Jesus told the parable of the lost coin. But there were so many parables that time, and Judas had listened with only one ear, the other reaching for the crowd reaction, weighing the whispers and the sighs, the half-spoken questions.

It was, he noticed, a parable that went over well, especially with the women. Jesus was defending His love for sinners. And He said:

"What woman, having ten drachmas, if she loses one, does not light a candle, and sweep the house, and search diligently till she finds it?"

A drachma was about the same as a Roman denarius, or penny—no trifling sum. It was a good day's wage, and, the way the times were, it took a family a long while to be able to put away even one drachma. To lose one out of ten was a serious emergency.

Every woman in that crowd, and her husband, knew the urgency of that search. To light a candle in the daytime was extravagant, but necessary in the nearly windowless room of an average house. A coin might roll into any corner, get lost under the straw laid on the earthen floor, lie unseen in a coating of dust to be trod underfoot. What if the animals, the chickens and sheep which at night sheltered in the doorways within breathing distance of the family, should snuffle and peck at the coin? There were so many ways for the money to disappear forever.

Jesus Himself seemed to be remembering back to the days of His own childhood, when Joseph would bring home the coins he earned with his saw and hammer, and Mary would keep the money safe in a purple earthenware jar. Coins had been lost in that household too. And even those who are not slaves to money must take care of the goods God gives them. Joseph had had a horror of waste. . . .

"And when she has found it," continued Jesus, "she will call together her friends and neighbors, saying: 'Rejoice with me, because I have found the coin which I had lost!'"

The men grunted. Wasn't it just like a woman to let the whole world in on her business? The women shrugged. There were few enough things to rejoice over. The recovery of a whole drachma would do nicely. That was the trouble with men—they did not appreciate the importance of little things!

But Jesus commanded their attention.

"So I say to you—there shall be joy before the angels of God upon *one sinner* doing penance."

One sinner! That was it. The importance of *one*—not of a nation, not of a whole people, but of one soul lost and found. As He looked into your eyes you knew that He would have come for your sake and yours alone. You felt that because God had minted your soul personally you were a coin of near infinite importance to Jesus.

Yet it was not strategy, not a technique. It was the love of God in action. The secret of the universe stood before them, the overwhelming fact that God did so love each soul that He had sent His only begotten Son to redeem them.

He turned those utterly deep dark eyes of love on each one. Judas met them, and even in the noon sun a shiver passed down his arms. For a moment he wondered if he had misgauged this Master, if perhaps the kingdom of God would not be as he had thought.

What puzzled him was in the look of sadness on that face, as if Jesus were searching in him for something that was lost. . . .

27

THE STEWARD WHO CHEATED HIS LORD*

H<small>E HAD</small> sometimes the look a grownup wears watching children concoct the numberless rules and details of make-believe. There is, you know, exhausting seriousness to the challenges of playing house, of jumping rope, endless backward and forward steps to be taken, formulas and rhymes to be repeated quite properly before you can win the game.

He had the half-amused, half-puzzled look of a father as He walked the streets of the city, watching and listening. The bazaars were crowded with bargaining and arguing, men buying melons and Jaffa oranges, linens and oils and sugar water, sheep and chickens and perfume. Men plotted and planned and schemed and laughed. Women talked and gossiped and whispered and laughed. And everyone was busy making his way in the world.

And night would come, and they would sleep, and tomorrow they would be busy again with the same things.

Jesus watched. And the Twelve watched Him. They had expected to see nothing but scorn for such affairs. Instead they saw a kind of fascination, a kind of reluctant admiration,

* Luke 16:1–9.

as if there were a great lesson to be learned here. And they did not understand.

It was then that He told them the most puzzling of all the parables, the story of the steward who cheated his master.

"There was," He said, "a certain rich man who had a steward. And it was reported to him that the steward had been squandering and wasting his wealth."

That was a common enough situation. Right in this bazaar a man could probably find a steward who had been trusted to manage an estate and instead ran it to please himself. Some were known to live more royally than their own masters. Others devised schemes to sell their masters' property cheaply to their own families and friends, to pad payrolls and expense accounts. There is nothing new in graft today.

"And," said Jesus, "he called his steward and said to him: 'What is this I hear about you? Give me an account of your stewardship, for you cannot be my steward any longer!'"

Dismissal was the least punishment he deserved. Of course, it would not be easy for him to get another job. And a man like that would find unemployment most difficult!

Jesus nodded. "And the steward said to himself:

"'What am I going to do, now that my lord has taken the stewardship away from me? To dig I am not able. To beg I am ashamed.'"

The Twelve almost laughed. Their Master, caught up in His own story, had become for the moment another man. He stood before them as the steward—shrewd, fastidious, and distressed. Then across His face flashed a gleam of cleverness, and in the proper voice of the steward He said:

"'I know what I shall do! For when I am removed from my stewardship, then they will receive me into their houses!'"

The Twelve looked up questioningly. And Jesus continued:

"So he called together every one of his lord's debtors. And he said to the first:

"'How much do you owe my lord?'

"And he said: 'A hundred barrels of oil.'

"The steward said to him: 'Take your bill, and sit down quickly, and write—fifty!'

"Then he said to another: 'And how much do you owe?'

"He said: 'A hundred quarter measures of wheat.'

"The steward said: 'Take your bill and write—eighty!'"

Jesus stopped. The Twelve pursed their lips and looked at each other. It was a clever scheme. Dishonest, unjust—but clever. A bit of foresight, a touch of prudent juggling, the refusal to accept defeat, and the steward had won himself friends who would take care of him after he was jobless. He had played one against the other in a plan that would delight the hearts of many a Jerusalem businessman.

But, coming from Jesus, the idea was extraordinary. Frankly, they had not thought Him capable of even inventing such skulduggery. They did not realize yet how intimately He knew the ways of men, for evil as well as good.

Of course, thought James, in the parable the lord will undoubtedly find out he has been cheated, and then . . .

"And the lord," said Jesus, "praised the unjust steward, because he had acted wisely."

Even Matthew's bright black eyes blinked in amazement. Praise a crooked steward? Call it wisdom to deceive and cheat?

"The children of this world," said Jesus, "are wiser in their own generation and ways than the children of light in theirs. And I say to you—make friends for yourselves with the mammon of iniquity, so that when you fail they may receive you into the everlasting dwellings."

He fell silent, leaving the Twelve in utter bewilderment.

Then slowly, with His help, they found their way to the inner truth of that strange story, a truth that lives still today.

The lord praised the steward—*his* master, not Jesus, commended him. And he praised the steward not for his dishonesty but for his worldly wisdom, for the prudence of scheming to take care of himself.

And the lesson Jesus wants us to learn is not from the example of dishonesty but from the determined busy zeal of the steward's self-preservation. If only—He is saying—the children of light would be half as busy protecting their future in heaven as the children of the world are in protecting their hides and fortunes!

Around Jesus and His twelve children of light swirled the swarm of children of the world—busy, busy, busy earning their earthly future. In their generation—unredeemed by grace, trained in astute business dealings—they were consumed with zeal. But the children of light in the new generation of Christ were supposed to be just as busy about heavenly things. And they were supposed to use all the energy and cleverness and intelligence God gave them to protect themselves in grace.

What did Jesus mean for us to learn?

He might come today and point to some international racketeer and ask us to realize that, if we worked as hard for good as he did for the evil of dope peddling or smuggling or gambling, then we would be great in the kingdom of light as he is in the kingdom of darkness.

He might come and speak of a successful businessman. He might say, "Look at the time he spends studying for his vocation, at the hours he spends at meetings and conventions to prepare himself for advancement. He uses his free time to entertain the men who may help him get ahead. His theater dates, his dinners, his games are all designed to increase his chance of worldly success. He is willing to bribe or threaten his way to the top. As a child of the world he is an expert.

"But," He might say, "look at those who intend to claim the kingdom of heaven. How much time do they spend on gaining that treasure? Do they give one hour a week to church and consider that too much? Do they seek out the souls who can best help them to union with God? Will they sit up nights studying to understand their new business, giving all their energy to develop the spirit of prayer? Compared to the child of the world, they are idiots and failures in their own chosen field!"

The one career that matters is our career with God. Everything else should come second. To that vocation we should give our keenest talents—and we do not.

And if in the day of reckoning we are found to have misused and squandered the fortune of which the Lord made us stewards, then what?

"Make friends for yourselves with the mammon of iniquity," He said.

"Mammon" was an Aramaic word much like our word "lucre." It was used with the words "iniquity" or "unrighteousness" as we use the cliché "filthy lucre." But why should a follower of Christ make friends with filthy lucre?

What did the steward do in the parable? He won friends and advocates by his use of the power he was about to lose. And we are to do the same, on a different plane, in the world of the spirit.

Take the money that is yours, He was saying, whatever little it may be, and give it in alms to the poor. Take the spiritual treasury that is yours, the riches of grace and of prayer, and give it to others. If you fail, they may still plead for you, still take you with them into the everlasting dwellings of the kingdom.

Even to the Twelve, at first hearing it was a startling teaching. It seemed almost mercenary and cheap, a way of scheming to bargain your way into heaven. In the same way today there are people who consider it somehow beneath their dignity to *work* their way into heaven. Like a proud family come down in the world, they would rather take their chances and starve than act like human beings and start climbing the ladder. They are, actually, far less realistic than Christ about this business of earning heaven.

It was, probably, Matthew who grasped the parable first— Matthew who had lived in service of the mammon of iniquity before the call of Christ.

The trouble with us, thought Matthew, is that we think the world and heaven are so far apart that we cannot see how the ways of one can fit into the other. But Jesus did not ask me to forget all I learned as a tax collector when He called me to be a disciple. He asked me only to change my goal, to use all my wits and strength in His service. He asked me to transform what was already in me in this new life, this new generation. After all, thought Matthew, heaven is not for idiots or for lazy souls. It takes every bit of energy and cleverness we have.

Ambition in itself is not wrong. The world seethes with ambition for mammon, and that is wrong. But we must remember that we must also be consumed by ambition—the proper virtuous ambition to serve God and achieve heaven. It is an ambition that demands that we use our heads. As a child transfers the seriousness of his make-believe to the problems of the adult world, just so must we transfer ours to the challenge of heaven.

28

LAZARUS AND THE RICH MAN[*]

HE WAS dressed as a poor man, in a tunic, a cloak, turban, and sandals. More than two years now He had been a wayfarer, journeying with His Twelve. He had come this month into the land called Perea, east of the Dead Sea. He had no caravan, no entourage, no luggage, though He was far from home.

And those who listened to Him here in the shade of the palms knew this Man owned nothing. One of the Twelve did carry the combined treasury of them all. Judas, his name was. But from the look and sound of it the leather purse could not boast more than a few coins.

Yet this Jesus carried Himself like a king, as if His hands —spread now in telling gesture—controlled the wealth of nations.

Not only was He poor. He found dignity in being poor. He rejoiced in having nothing. He even asked men to turn their backs on the things of this world to follow Him.

No one had ever before been proud of being poor.

His listeners, most of them, knew the bony hand of poverty. Taxes, illness, exorbitant interest on loans snatched hard-earned coins from them. Their robes were patched, their

* Luke 16:19–31.

hands twisted with callus. Some were bitter, some resigned to the will of heaven. But this Jesus seemed to honor poverty.

Men remembered when, two years before, not far from this spot, John the Baptist had been executed. And they remembered the strange list of signs this Jesus had sent to John as proof of His mission. He had listed miracles, but He had climaxed His credentials with these unforgettable words:

"Behold, the poor have the gospel preached to them!"

This very afternoon, preaching to the poor, He had said:

"You cannot serve God and mammon!" You cannot serve God and chase after success and riches too.

The crowd had murmured and shifted on their haunches, and wondered. For years men had thought that God rewarded the good with fortune on earth. If you were wealthy it was because your virtue had pleased God. A successful harvest, a flourishing trade, were blessings from on high, and they belonged to those God loved. The poor were not only miserable, they were also obviously not worthy of God's blessings.

The Pharisees taught that. And there were Pharisees in this crowd of listeners here in Perea. They were everywhere He went these days, conspicuous in their rich outer robes, their linen tunics. Perfumed cloths protected their noses from the aroma of His lesser followers. Pharisees dogged His footsteps heroically, official observers for the Temple in Jerusalem, sacrificing comfort and peace to document reports on this rabble-rousing heretic.

They had heard Him stab at the love of money before. And they considered the praise of poverty a highly explosive doctrine. They derided Him now publicly.

"Is it not possible to be rich and good at the same time?" laughed one, wafting his oiled handkerchief before him.

Jesus, in silence, seemed to say that it was—possible.

"Do not Moses and the prophets tell us that all good things come from God? And that He smiles on the virtuous and blesses their undertakings by making them rich?" asked another Pharisee.

And they managed to convey the idea, without being so rude as to say so directly, that anyone with eyes could answer that question. After all, they, the Pharisees, were known to be superbly religious men. And they were not poor. As for this vagabond Preacher and the Twelve—well?

With an eloquent shrug, a lift of a scholarly eyebrow, they lined up Scripture on their side and leaned back with a smile and a sigh.

But Jesus said, so quietly that the words were almost lost in the shuffling of sandals and the tree rustle in the breeze overhead:

"You try to justify yourselves before men. But God knows your hearts. For what men raise up as high and mighty is an abomination before God."

And He began then to tell a story, a parable, and a silence came over them all as they listened.

"There was a certain rich man," He said, "who was dressed in purple and fine linen, and feasted sumptuously every day."

A Perean farmer, debt-ridden and watery-eyed, cocked a grin at the Pharisee near him.

"And there was a certain beggar, named Lazarus, who lay outside his gate, full of sores, hoping to be filled with the crumbs that fell from the rich man's table. And the dogs came and licked his sores."

Like all His parables, this began with an everyday affair. Beggars were more common than dogs in Palestine. The sick, the crippled, the very old had no choice but to beg. And the rich looked on them as a normal nuisance, like a swarm of flies.

"And it came to pass that the beggar died—and was carried by angels into Abraham's bosom. And the rich man also died, and he was buried in hell."

The Pharisees coughed delicately into their handkerchiefs. The farmers and tradesmen grinned. This was fighting fire with fire! Everyone knew that the holiest and most just of men went to rest with Abraham, father of all the chosen people, the friend of God. And Jesus was answering the Pharisees and their pious references to Moses with Abraham—and a rich man burning in hell.

But the story was not over. Jesus still spoke in the same deep-pitched young voice:

"And the rich man, lifting his eyes in the torments of hell, saw Abraham far off, with Lazarus in his bosom, and he cried:

"'Father Abraham, have mercy on me! Send Lazarus just to dip the tip of his finger in water to cool my tongue, for I am tormented in this flame!'"

Men nudged each other with elbows, and hidden smiles. The rich man turned beggar, pleading for help from Lazarus!

"And Abraham said to him: 'Son, remember that you in your lifetime received good things, and Lazarus evil. But now he is comforted and you are tormented. And besides, between us and you there is fixed a great gulf so that anyone who wanted to go from here to you could not, nor can anyone come here from there.'"

Men closed their eyes at the thought of the endlessness of hell and the chasm that cut it off from heaven.

The voice of Jesus went on, deeper now, sad with warning:

"And the rich man said: 'Then, Father, I beg you, send Lazarus to my father's house where my five brothers live. Let him testify to them, lest they also come to this place of torments.'

"And Abraham said to him: 'They have Moses and the prophets. Let them hear them!'

"But he said: 'No, Father Abraham—but if one went to them from the dead, then they will do penance.'

"And Abraham said: 'If they do not hear Moses and the prophets, neither will they believe if one came back from the dead!'"

One by one heads turned to study the Pharisees in their discomfiture. A poor Man had told a parable—would one of them dare answer?

For all their intellectual airs, the Pharisees were not the only experts in Scripture. Every decent Jewish boy studied in the synagogue schools. The poor knew the Law too. And in this afternoon's shade the memories of old lessons sprang out with new emphasis. The Book of Deuteronomy, Moses' book, laid down the law that the rich must give to the poor. The prophets, too, had hammered the truth home. Isaias had said: "Deal your bread to the hungry, and bring the needy into your house. . . . Then the glory of the Lord shall gather you up."

Yet always, obstinately, men preferred to forget the divine command of charity. They had the Law written for all to read and know. They needed no miracle, no apparition to teach them. They needed only the miracle of the heart to realize that money is a gift to be used for God, not a reward to be clutched in privacy.

Then, as stillness stretched like a covering over them all, the heads slowly turned back to face Jesus. And in the face of that poorest of men the poor learned a lesson for themselves.

Compared to Lazarus, they were rich. They at least enjoyed the dignity and honor of earning their own bread. They were not helpless, not shamed into beggary. And they too were responsible to God as the rich man was, for the use of their own wealth. So long as there was one man in need, they too would be bound by the Law to help him.

Or, like the rich man, they might find themselves beggars in the next world, beggars without hope of alms.

The Law, this Jesus was saying, was not for the rich or for the poor—but for men and their souls, without regard to their place in this world. Not all who are rich are friends of God. Neither does poverty automatically make you holy. What matters is to set your heart not on the goods of this world but on the true riches of eternity.

Were He talking to us today, He might have used a different story. No one today lies patiently at a rich man's front steps, waiting to be fed. You and I are not faced with the decision to march past a beggar every time we go in and out of our homes. We may meet one on the street. But our beggars are quickly bundled off to county homes or to jail. The state cares for them.

But He might instead show us the leprous child of India, the native of Kenya, the abandoned half-caste orphans of wars around the globe. He might pick from our wastebaskets the appeal of a hospital, the letter from a missionary. He might lead us to a dirty dark place in the city, where our antiseptic noses never have ventured, and ask us what we have done, what we have given of ourselves.

We can forget our beggars, lose sight of them in the hustle of growing savings accounts and insurance and a nice dinner for Sundays. But they lie at the gates of our hearts.

And we may someday lift our eyes to see them with Abraham in the arms of Christ Himself—the poor in body united to the One Who was poor in spirit, having spent Himself in love.

We must spend ourselves in love too. For before God we are all beggars of mercy. Yet, by His infinite goodness, we are rich—in grace.

29

THE UNPROFITABLE SERVANTS[*]

THE ONE thing He almost never gave them was praise. It was also one thing He would never accept for Himself.

He had majesty. He walked like a king, with inborn full awareness of Himself. No one who met Him could fail to feel that here was a Person like no other on earth. Like Him or hate Him, you could not remain indifferent to that impact of holiness.

He had in Him such a natural authority that all kinds of people, from a Roman army officer with a sick boy to a woman of the streets, would understand that when He spoke He expected to be obeyed. He taught with complete assurance. And He told the world clearly that it must recognize Him as the Son of God as well as of man, and that in Him alone could be found everlasting life.

Yet a humbler Personality was not to be found. He had absolutely no pride.

He had come to conquer the earth, to establish the kingdom of heaven. No Caesar, no Alexander, no Napoleon ever had such a mission—or such an opponent—as Jesus of Nazareth. He declared war on evil and death, and staked His

[*] Luke 17:5–10.

claim over the souls of all men of all time—as their Master, their Savior, and their Judge.

This was the nearly infinite task He had taken on Himself. And He treated it as a job to be done like any other, a service to be performed with every ounce of strength and love.

Nothing so puzzled the disciples as this humility of their Master. After all, the world knew that for a man to succeed as a leader he must be driven by ambition. People understood that geniuses and rulers have to be self-centered, egotistic, eccentric. It was only by insisting on his self-importance that a man rose to the top.

And Jesus was not like that.

Worship, adoration, the homage of a crowd that recognized Him as the Messiah—these He would accept. To refuse would have been to deny His divinity. What kind of God would simper behind false modesty?

But He accepted also abuse and threats of mob violence, insult and ingratitude—and went about His business.

The disciples followed Him. A disciple, after all, must try to be like his master. And the Twelve tried. In the months since they had wrenched themselves violently from the quiet routine of home and daily trade they had taken His every command to heart—from going without ready cash in their belts to valiantly forgiving their enemies. They had learned the new ways to pray and to think of God. They had come to accept hunger and thirst and the dusty feet of travel and the long hours of dealing with crowds of the sick and the desperate as a career certain to be rewarded.

They were not the same men they had been. And yet the moment they began to take pride in their progress Jesus would turn and look at them—and they would wither into silence.

There were times, thought Philip, when He made you feel

like an overgrown, clumsy, swell-headed fool. A kinder man never lived, but He had no patience with self-esteem. And He destroyed it, ripped it from you not by what He said or did but just by being Himself. His own humility, clear-eyed and serene, made you feel, thought Philip, as if you were tripping over your own feet trying to follow Him.

Take the matter of working miracles.

Jesus had given all twelve of His disciples the power to heal and cure and to cast out unclean spirits. He had sent them to preach and to work miracles. And soberly, with the fear of God trembling in their souls, they had gone to the cities of Israel and done as they were told.

It was a heady sensation—to make a leper's skin fresh and new, to give a crippled child the power to walk. They knew, because He had told them, that they were only instruments of the Holy Spirit, tools and servants of God. But still it was a thrilling thing to know God was using you.

It seemed as good a proof as any that you could be proud of yourself, certain that you were pleasing Him!

And then, to their confusion, they found that their miraculous powers did not always work. A man brought a child to be healed, a little boy suffering from epileptic seizures that had toppled him into the fire more than once, and into the river till he almost drowned. The disciples laid their hands on the boy and prayed—and nothing happened.

But Jesus, when the child was brought to Him, cured him at once.

Later, when the crowds had thinned, and they could speak to Him alone, the Twelve asked Jesus:

"Why were we not able to cure the child? What was the matter?"

And though they did not say so in as many words, they were also asking why He had let them face such humiliation in public. Was that the thanks they got, for Him to take their power away at such a time?

A smile lurked deep behind His brown eyes. He saw the sting of embarrassment on their cheeks.

"If you had faith," He said, "faith like a grain of mustard seed, you might say to this mulberry tree: 'Be uprooted and be transplanted into the sea!'—and it would obey you."

Faith? They had faith. They believed in God and in Jesus Christ, Son of the living God. But perhaps it was not enough, not even as great as a mustard seed. Well, if it was faith they lacked for success, if their failure in the eyes of the public was due to a lack of faith, then:

"Lord—increase our faith!"

Jesus stood, His chin down, His eyes studying the ground, rocking a bit on His bare heels. And He answered them in a roundabout way, a gentle way, with the parable of the unprofitable servants.

"Which one of you," He said, "if you had a servant plowing a field, or feeding cattle, would say to him when he came in from the field: 'Go at once and sit down and eat'?"

He tilted His head to the left, smiling up under the heavy dark brows.

"Would you not say to him instead: 'Prepare my supper, and dress yourself to serve me while I eat and drink, and afterward you shall eat and drink'?"

Matthew, who had had some experience with servants, wrinkled his chin and nodded knowingly.

Jesus continued. "Does a man thank that servant for doing the things he commanded him? I think not!"

After all, thought the disciples, it wasn't a lack of politeness or gratitude to assume that a man would do his daily duties correctly. No one expected to be thanked for routine chores or for obeying the everyday orders of his employer.

For an act of heroism, perhaps, for something beyond and above the line of duty, a man would expect extra reward. If a servant made his master a fortune all on his own, he would deserve to be treated with honor. But it was an arrogant soul who would expect to be pampered for an ordinary job!

They nodded with understanding smiles. Then Jesus raised His head and said softly:

"So you also, when you shall have done all those things that are commanded you, shall say to yourselves: 'We are unprofitable servants. We have only done that which we ought to.'"

Unprofitable servants! The faces of the Twelve flushed at the words. Is that all He thinks we are, servants performing our duty and nothing more? Keeping the commandments may be all in a day's work, though even that is difficult enough to warrant some praise. But we are His chosen Twelve. And He relies on us rather specially. He gave us the power to work miracles, which is spectacular and profitable no matter how you look at it. And certainly we are doing more than ordinary servants. We bring Him profit—we add to His kingdom!

But the look on the Master's face silenced rebellion. It was the look of a king who has chosen to serve in the front lines, the look of the Lord Who would one evening wash the bare feet of these same Twelve.

Philip scraped his heel in the dust, a lock of black curls falling apologetically over his thin young forehead. To serve God, to obey His commands, was the greatest gift a man could be given—and they had almost forgotten it! Men boasted of the privilege of serving in a palace, but to be able to choose to serve Christ was an honor far more dizzying.

And suddenly they saw, these Twelve, that it made no difference what task you were given in the service of this King, so long as you worked with a good will. A servant of God might one day be called to work miracles before an admiring crowd, to minister to thousands, to convert a whole nation. And that was no cause for a swelled head. It was, literally, all in a day's work. The next day the same servant might be sent into the fields to plow or be put to scrubbing floors. It didn't matter where He sent you to work or what He gave you to do.

All that mattered was to serve, freely and whole-souledly— in loving surrender to God.

It would not be easy. It would seem to be the sure way to failure, the destruction of personality, debasing a freeborn man into an abject slave. Pride would see it as the road to death.

But at the head of the Twelve stood Jesus—Who came as a servant to do what His Father commanded, and Who would one day look back at His life and sum it up by saying:

"I have done His will in all things. . . ."

Philip raised shy brown eyes under thick lashes and saw His Master standing tall and free before him. And suddenly as never before he felt at ease with Jesus. When a man lets go the burden of pride his back straightens and his feet grow nimble and sure on the path.

Pride died that day in the market place among the echoes of the parable. And the power of truth took its place.

For those who loved and served God there would be few moments of glory and scant praise. But it would not matter.

After all, a disciple must try to be like his master—then and now.

30

THE WIDOW AND THE JUDGE*

H E LOOKED a bit like a father forced to send his children alone into danger, trying desperately to give them every last-minute piece of advice he could.

And, like children, they did not begin to understand the size of the danger they faced.

They had been told by Him that the kingdom of heaven would come and they were, if the truth were known, a little impatient for it. They could not see why the great God should have any trouble establishing His kingdom, and since they were to be part of it they wished He would hurry. It is a feeling shared by many even now.

He had told them again and again that He would suffer and be rejected. He had told them, "The kingdom of heaven is within you."

And still they looked for it to come in a fine blinding light of majesty, with a fanfare of angel song and themselves in proper distinction beside Jesus on a throne.

They felt, as many others since, that they had already followed Christ a long hard way and that it was about time they had their reward. They had endured obscurity and poverty, they had been laughed at and insulted, they had given

* Luke 18:1–8.

up everything for Him. True, they knew they could not be happy apart from Him. But a man would think, after all this time, something wonderful must be about to happen.

Yet the way Jesus looked did not augur a triumphal claiming of a kingdom in Jerusalem.

He carried with Him in these days a sense of eternity so vivid that you could almost breathe it. Walking with Him was like sailing the Sea of Galilee with a thunderhead building on one shore and a pale windless dawn on the other—or like walking beneath the edge of a cloud, in the frontier between rain and sun.

From the time they first met Him they had wondered at the strange mixture of majesty and camaraderie in Him. He had a dignity no swarm of children could destroy, unruffled by heckling or by midnight confidences. There was no doubt that He was by birth and right the Master. And yet at the same time He was young, scarcely older than the Twelve, with a zest for living and a ready humor.

These days He no longer laughed easily. They had journeyed in a long, seemingly random path, bound slowly for Jerusalem. And His face, changing in expression like the shadowed hollows of a mountain, seemed caught now in a grave sadness they could not explain.

He had just finished telling them of the last day, when the kingdom would come, the day when the Son of Man would be revealed. He had said that it would come without warning, as the flood came to the people of Noah's time, or the fire and brimstone to the people of Sodom. Men would eat and drink, buy and sell, plant and build, and suddenly the hour would come. And some would be taken to Christ and others would not.

He turned suddenly to them. His voice seemed to thrust itself into their hearts.

"Pray! Pray always, without stopping!"

He knew what they were thinking. He could see them sketching in their minds a wide easy road to the revelation of the last day. And He knew He must make it very clear that only prayer would carry them to the last day. Only by constant, untiring prayer would these Twelve and all the others after them ever reach the day of the coming of the kingdom.

Did they think the good followers of Christ would have a royal road? They would be persecuted and mistreated so seriously that they would cry out to God to avenge them on their enemies! Let no one think the way of Christ is easy. They must know before they started that it is a path of suffering and of injustice!

And that day Jesus told the Twelve, and told us too, the parable of the judge and the widow.

He said:

"There was a judge in a certain city who did not fear God and who had no respect for men either.

"And there was a certain widow in that city, and she came to him, saying: 'Do justice for me against my enemy!'"

A widow in Israel was about the most helpless of people, next to an orphan—they all knew that. Unless her husband's family was alive to take her in, or she had sons to care for her, she was a woman alone and could do nothing to defend herself unless the courts intervened. Jewish Law, which came from God Himself, was magnificently detailed in its justice, designed to protect those who could not help themselves. A good judge, taking the Law of God seriously, would rush to help the widow. But this judge was the worst possible.

"And he would not help her for a long time.

"But finally he said to himself: 'Though I do not fear God, or care about men, still because this widow is a nuisance to me I will see that justice is done for her—lest the way she continually comes to me wear me out!'"

The picture was clear. Peter, whose mother-in-law had been a widow living in his house after his wife died, could almost hear the woman in the parable heckling the judge. When you are helpless, as a widow is without a man, there is nothing to do but make a nuisance of yourself. And that widow probably waited at the judge's door, followed him down the street, pestered him in court, pulling at his sleeve night and day. No wonder he finally answered her!

But Jesus was not smiling.

"That is what the *unjust* judge said, and did.

"Then will not God do justice for His elect who cry to Him day and night?"

James, who more even than the others cherished Scripture, nodded. The Psalms called God "the father of orphans and the judge of widows." Placed against Him, the unjust judge was the perfect opposite. But if even a wicked man could not resist the constant prayer of the helpless, would God turn a deaf ear?

"And will God be patient forever with those who persecute His elect?" Jesus bent His own head as if in prayer. "I tell you that He will revenge them, quickly.

"But yet, when the Son of Man does come in His glory, do you think He shall find faith on earth?"

The sadness of His voice startled them.

He raised His deep-set eyes to meet theirs in silent challenge. It would take great faith to pray as the widow prayed, refusing to be unanswered, calling constantly for help.

Like the widow, the Christian must be humble enough to know that there is no other help except from the Judge. Like the widow, the Christian must wait for the time when that prayer will be met by action, undiscouraged, believing that God will take care of His own.

Peter shivered as he returned the Lord's steady gaze. He

was not a man used to begging, not the kind to throw pride to the breeze easily, even with God. And yet he saw that this must be—that in years to come he would have to cast himself on the mercy of God and wait in patience without ever ceasing to pray.

"Thy kingdom come," John whispered to himself. That was the way Jesus had taught them to pray. And it would be a petition repeated more often than the fall of waves on a shore, night and day for—who knows how long?

For an instant the Twelve understood. And in that moment they shared the yearning of Jesus for the world to grasp the truth of this. The way to the kingdom was hard and painful. More than once it would seem that God turned a blank ear to our helplessness, careless of what our enemies—the devil and his children—would do. We would be persecuted, we would be killed for faith. We would lose friends and honor and business by obeying God's laws. And it would seem there was no justice anywhere.

And we must keep our faith till the second coming of Christ. And we must, like the widow, never stop crying out for the Lord to help us.

One of those Twelve would become impatient with the slowness of God in making His kingdom come—so restless that he would throw away his faith and act on his own. And in every man's life there is a time when natural common sense insists that God no longer cares.

It takes uncommon sense, above nature, to have faith that God, unlike the wicked judge, has His own divine reasons for biding His time.

And uncommon perseverance to keep praying—like a child in the dark, like a sheep lost on the mountain, or like a widow seeking justice.

31

THE PHARISEE AND THE
PUBLICAN*

H E W A S a Master quite different from any other.

And the Twelve were getting tired of defending Him against the sneers of those who wondered how anyone could follow such an unimpressive, inferior kind of leader.

Even among themselves they wondered a bit about His lack of self-importance. It did not seem quite right. He would at times take His turn at cooking their meals, at stirring porridge or cutting bread and cheese. When one of the Twelve broke his walking staff, it was most often Jesus Who made a new one for him, because after all He was the only carpenter among them. He was quite likely to pick up what another man dropped, or hold a child for a mother who was tired.

He was in command. There was no doubt of that. And He had the dignity of a king. But He was also the quickest to serve, to help, to humble Himself.

And He did not look down on anyone. That was the strangest part about Him. He knew the faults of everyone. Had He not told the woman at the well in Samaria all the secrets of her life with one man after another? Yet He had spoken to her as courteously as to a queen. He had healed

* Luke 18:9–14.

men and gotten no thanks for it. He had seen a small army of His followers turn their backs and leave Him after He told them of the Bread of Heaven. He had been attacked physically, and jeered out of His own home town.

None of that seemed to faze Him. Neither did praise.

When the crowd had tried to make Him their king, after He multiplied the loaves and fishes, He had simply disappeared—just as He had done when another crowd in another place had tried to kill Him.

He seemed to be without pride. He did not seem to care at all what people thought of Him.

And He prayed constantly, in silence and in words. He asked the Father to help Him. He said always that without the Father He could do nothing.

It was very confusing. Certainly no greater man ever lived than this Jesus Who could and did say also that He was the Son of God.

And yet He was also the most humble of persons.

People usually, thought James, show their strength by insisting on their rights. Even God on Mount Sinai made His power quite clear. He was unapproachable! And men on earth vie with each other for first place in dignity, for extra trappings on their clothes, for the best in food and comfort and attention. But Jesus was acting as neither God nor man was known to act.

"The last shall be first," He had said. . . . "Take the lowest place.". . . "He who humbles himself shall be exalted.". . .

And then, on that last long journey to Jerusalem, He told them a parable, a tale of a Pharisee and a publican.

Every one of the Twelve knew intimately what Jesus thought of both Pharisees and publicans in general.

Matthew, after all, had been a publican—one of the most

hated men in Palestine, a Jewish tax collector in the service of Rome. Publicans were hated then the way collaborationists were hated during World War II, because they chose to make their living serving the conqueror. They were also believed to be thoroughly dishonest—and many publicans did indeed have sticky fingers and secret pockets. A publican in the mind of the people was a cross between a teacher's pet, a traitor, and a gyp artist. He was not a very popular fellow.

But Jesus had come one day to the toll booth where a publican named Levi was doing business, and called him from his coins and tallies. A publican became one of the Twelve—the saint we call Matthew!

The Pharisees, on the other hand, were the most respectable of fellows, the spiritual upper class. The name "Pharisee" meant "separated," and they considered themselves quite correctly separated from the run-of-the-street Jews, who were obviously incapable of pleasing God. Only a Pharisee, said the Pharisees, could understand God's Law fully or pray properly. They were experts in religion. And they were entirely self-sufficient.

The Pharisees did not approve of Jesus. And He did not approve of them.

Just a week before this day He had told the Pharisees outright that they were hypocrites, moneygrubbers, arrogant, and blind. "An abomination before God," He called them. And they called Him a glutton, a wine drinker, and a man who consorted with sinners—which did not bother Jesus at all.

Now, in the last days before He went again to Jerusalem, He was teaching His disciples the science of prayer. He had told them they must pray constantly, with a faith nothing could swerve.

But this faith, He said, must be in God—not in themselves!

"Two men went up into the Temple to pray—one a Pharisee, the other a publican," said Jesus.

"The Pharisee, standing, prayed this way in his heart:

" 'O God, I give Thee thanks that I am not like other men—extortioners, unjust, adulterers—like this publican!' "

Jude grinned. How often they had all heard the daily prayer prescribed by the Pharisees: "Bless God, for He has not made me a Gentile. Bless God, for He has not made me a woman. Bless God, for He has not made me a servant." The parable's Pharisee was running true to form.

Jesus continued, in the voice of the Pharisee:

" 'I fast twice a week. I give tithes of all that I possess.' "

And in the Master's mimicry they could see plainly the Pharisee laying his credentials before God, proving beyond doubt his worthiness to be heard. A more self-satisfied tone you could not imagine.

"And the publican, standing way back, would not even dare lift his eyes to heaven. But he struck his breast, saying: 'O God, be merciful to me, a sinner.' "

Jesus put His hand lightly on Matthew's shoulder.

"I say to you that man went home justified with God rather than the other. Because everyone who exalts himself shall be humbled, and he that humbles himself shall be exalted."

In the silence the Twelve heard the echo of the night when He had dined with the Pharisees in Perea and teased them about their rivalry for first place at table, the night He had told the parable about the great supper. They heard too His voice on the mountainside so long before, pronouncing the Beatitudes. *Blessed are the poor in spirit. Blessed are the meek.*

It is not human nature to be humble.

But it is in the nature of those who love and live with God.

How many times had Jesus taught them the lesson of humility? Even from His lips once was not enough. Still James and John would squabble over who was to have the higher place in heaven. Still Peter would not have learned enough to keep from protesting when Jesus submitted to the indignity of arrest. Pride blooms high in the best of men.

And yet it was plain Jesus wanted these who loved Him to defy their own pride—to go against human nature with the help of grace.

The Son of God was born in a cave for animals, raised in poverty, earning His bread with His own hands, refusing all temptation to earthly glory. He Who alone had the right to be exalted humbled Himself, a prince in disguise.

And He looked at the Twelve that day with challenge searing His great brown eyes—"Dare you to do what I will not do?"

Peter lowered his head. He glimpsed then a truth about man's dealing with God—a truth men still find it hard to remember. There is no one who can stand before the infinite good God and claim to be anything at all. Not one of us on our own merits has even the right to speak to Him. And until we realize first-heart our own nothingness we are really walling ourselves off from God with pride. He cannot help us as long as we believe we can help ourselves. Like a baby refusing help on the stairs, we will fall flat on our faces. But if we admit to Him and to ourselves that alone we can do nothing, He will come and lift us up beside Him. It's as simple as that—and as difficult for pride to do.

That is why, the holier a soul is, the more wretched and sinful it considers itself. St. Teresa of Avila, who climbed the mountains of mysticism, said she did not know anyone more worthless and wicked than herself. St. Francis of Assisi said that, next to God, he was a worm. They were not exaggerating or posing. They meant it. As Francis said, the beginning of wisdom is in knowing Who God is—and who you are.

We have our Pharisees today, you know, the people who keep a mental score card of their virtues and good works all ready to impress God. They are very glad indeed that they are not drunkards in the gutter, or cheats, or adulterers like some people they could mention. They make sure the world knows how austerely they treat themselves. And they give fine showy contributions to the proper charities.

And they have no idea what a surprise is in store for them when they meet their Lord face to face!

The Twelve were still a long way from learning the lesson completely. But as they looked at Him that day they realized that in a real sense it was His humility that made Him the perfect Master that He was.

It was a backwards kind of truth—that by lowering yourself you rise, by taking the last place you become first. But as the world would see later, all of Christianity was a contradiction. Through death comes life, through sacrifice comes gain, through the Cross comes heaven.

It comes down to one thing—the difference between the purely human life and God's life. And they are worlds apart.

32

THE TALENTS*

HE CERTAINLY did not seem to be what you might call a practical man.

He had, it is true, managed a small carpentry shop well enough to provide for His mother and put away funds to keep her after He left home. But now, in the days of His preaching, He seemed to take no thought at all for the next day, let alone the next year. He was frugal about small things, insisting that not a scrap of bread or fish be wasted. But He seemed almost irresponsible about big things.

What could you do with a Man who found His tax money in a fish's mouth as if it were the perfectly logical place for it to come from? Or who was willing to nibble raw grain from a field or figs from a tree rather than budget and plan ahead?

Most of the Twelve by now were just about convinced that Jesus believed not only that poverty was an honor but that it was wrong to make any effort to produce anything. Some of them, remembering that once He had told them to meditate on the lilies of the field, had begun to feel that to please God you had only to drift through life like a flower petal.

They did not understand.

And, as so often, it seemed that He read their thoughts

* Matthew 25:14–29; Luke 19:12–26.

that afternoon as they rested in the olive grove on the mount outside Jerusalem. He answered them with a parable, the unforgettable story of the talents.

"A man was going away to a distant country," He said. "And he called his servants and gave them some of his wealth.

"To one he gave five talents. And to another, two. And to another, one—to each according to his ability. And then immediately he left."

Peter wrinkled his forehead in calculation. A talent was a small fortune, equal to about a thousand Greek drachmas. In American money it would be about fifteen hundred dollars for the lowest servant, three thousand for the second, and seventy-five hundred for the most skilled. That was a great deal to trust to stewards, no matter how faithful they were! Peter sucked his lower lip and wondered what a man would do with that much money in his care.

"He that was given the five talents," said Jesus thoughtfully, "went his way and traded with them, and made a profit of five talents more.

"And the man who was given two also invested them and earned another two.

"But he that was given one talent went and dug a hole in the ground and hid his lord's money."

He paused, looking slowly from one to another of the Twelve. He saw Matthew, who obviously admired the wise investors who doubled the money. And He saw those who seemed to think that perhaps the safest thing to do with someone else's money was to bury it.

Then Jesus continued: "But after a long time the lord of those servants came and reckoned accounts with them.

"And the one who received the five talents came to him, bringing the other five talents, and said: 'Lord, you gave me five talents, and see—I have gained another five over and above that.'

"His lord said to him: 'Well done, good and faithful servant! Because you have been faithful over a few things, I will place you in trust over many things. You shall enter into your lord's joy.'"

Matthew nodded. He had not been sure so apparently unworldly a person as Jesus would see things that way, and it pleased him to hear it.

"And the man who received the two talents came," said Jesus, "and said: 'Lord, you gave me two talents, and see—I have gained another two.'

"His lord said to him: 'Well done, good and faithful servant! Because you have been faithful over a few things, I will place you over many things. You shall enter into your lord's joy.'"

Jesus drew a deep breath and then went on:

"But he who received the one talent came and said: 'Lord, I know that you are a hard man.'" Jesus' voice, so nimble in its mimicry, was pitched now in a half whine, treading close to sarcasm and insult as He spoke for the third servant. "'You—uh—reap where you have not sown, and you garner where you have not winnowed. And—uh—being afraid, I went and hid your talent in the ground. See—I give back to you what is yours!'"

The Twelve grinned. The Master's caricature was so apt, they could see and hear that sly servant flirting with danger as he spoke to the lord of the estate.

"And," continued Jesus, "his lord, answering, said to him:

"'Wicked, slothful servant! So you knew that I reap where I do not sow and gather where I have not winnowed—still you should therefore have given my money to the bankers.

Then when I came I would at least have had my own with interest!'"

Then Jesus, acting the role of the lord of the estate, seemed to turn to other servants, and in a voice of terrible doom said:

"'Take away from him the talent and give it to the one who has ten talents! For to everyone who has shall be given, and he shall have much. But from him that has not, even that which he seems to have shall be taken away.

"'And throw the unprofitable servant into the outer darkness. There shall be weeping and gnashing of teeth!'"

Peter, quite frankly, scratched his graying curls in puzzlement. It seemed a tremendous punishment for a small thing. And he was not even certain why it should be so wrong. You could, he thought, call it prudence to bury the money. There was no risk involved. Suppose the first two had invested their talents and lost, instead of gaining?

Even Matthew was startled. And Simon, the one they called the Zealot, had thought perhaps Jesus would praise the man with one talent for refusing to dabble in investments. Jesus had more than once criticized the rich. And what the servant had said, though not tactful, was apt to be true. Most rich men became rich not through their own labor but by raking in the profits of other men's work—a practice open to challenge then and now.

But Jesus simply watched the Twelve and smiled. And slowly, in the silence of the garden, they came to the truth of that amazing story.

The lord, obviously, was God. And the talents were His gifts of grace and of natural ability given to all His servants— to some more, to some less. And they were given to be used, not to be left idle.

Every man is a servant, a steward of God, holding in trust the gold and silver of heaven. Everything is His—and we are to use what He gives us to spread His kingdom and advance His interests. To some He has given strength or beauty, to others artistic ability, to some business acumen. Some sow, some labor, some dream, some build. The gifts of the soul are even more varied, far richer. And there is no one who has not received the wealth of God.

To bury God's gifts is a sin without excuse. Just as a rich man expects his money to work for him, so God demands that His gifts increase in the hands of His servants, to be returned to Him with interest.

Peter, lost in thought, nodded. Who could call the Lord exacting or despotic for wanting His own profits? What did He do with them? He shared them with His servants. And the faithful steward wanted only to see the Lord's kingdom increase! There was risk, yes. But it was laziness, not prudence, that buried a talent in the ground. It was the refusal to serve—the backward sin of pride.

And, thought Simon the Zealot, from the one who has nothing even what he seems to have is taken away. In life it works that way. A talent not used fades and atrophies to uselessness. A man's muscles weaken, a woman's voice grows rusty, a soul's ability to pray and love dulls and withers. What you do not use you are not entitled to have. What you use for the glory of God will increase. In the realm of the spirit the rich do get richer and the poor poorer—and rightly so.

But, thought Matthew, it's a bit like taxes. The more you have, the more you are responsible for. The lord would not have been so pleased with the steward of five talents if he had made the same profit as the one with two! The greater your gifts from God, the greater the account demanded. There was no room for halfhearted service in the kingdom of heaven.

The Master lay resting under the trees, for all the world

like a vagabond. Yet, watching, they knew that here was the hardest-working man of all time, the One who used each talent to the utmost for the glory of God. Every moment of every day He offered, sanctifying it with love and service. Even in rest He gave glory!

It was not enough, He was saying, to avoid sin, to be so afraid of the world that you wrap yourself up in a hole and refuse to do anything.

Was ever a man less like a lily of the field? This Jesus' heels were callused from walking, forcing Himself from town to town to preach and to heal, to comfort and to encourage. Risk? Look down from this garden to the Temple of Jerusalem and see how He has gambled His talents against the power of the men who would murder Him. This was no idle wanderer. This was the most eminently practical Man Who lived, the One Who knew the precise value of every moment in the plans of God. He was concerned with riches that could not be seen.

In the Lord's kingdom there are no paupers except self-made ones—the result of wickedness and sloth. But there are many rich in grace who took God's gifts and used them for Him. And in the day of reckoning every living soul must account for what he has done with the talents that were his fortune.

33

THE ELEVENTH HOUR[*]

H E LOOKED for all the world like a gentleman inspecting his estates as He strode the dirt road up from the Jordan Valley to Jerusalem. He walked alone, ahead of the Twelve, His cheeks glowing with the fresh hillside wind.

He had the habit of living in the moment. What had happened ten minutes before, be it miracle or grief, was over. He was superbly focused in the present, tuned not to time but to timelessness. The young man had come and talked to Him and gone his way. Now Jesus was going His, through the land where the first promise of spring already reddened the slim branches.

The Twelve did not have His gift of dwelling in the moment. And they could not forget the young man. They were still puzzling over his meeting with the Master.

The young man was, they knew, very rich. He had come to ask Jesus what to do to earn life everlasting. He did keep the commandments. He was by men's standards a very good young man. But Jesus had laid down a condition he could not accept.

"If you will be perfect," Jesus had said, "go sell what you have and give to the poor, and you shall have treasure in

[*] Matthew 20:1–16.

heaven. And come, follow Me!" But the young man, who had great possessions, had gone away sadly.

Now Peter said, "We were not rich, but we did leave everything to follow Jesus—our boats, our businesses, our homes. What, I wonder, will our reward be?"

With Peter, thought always stumbled headlong into action. The others might have waited. Peter would ask Jesus now. He lumbered up ahead, trying to match his stride to the Master's lithe one.

"Look," he said, "we have left all things and followed You. What, therefore, shall we have?"

A smile of affectionate amusement crossed Jesus' face. Then He clasped a strong hand on Peter's shoulder, swung off the road, and settled under an olive tree as if He had long planned to rest a moment in this exact place and talk.

The Twelve sat around Him, men who had walked and talked with Him for over a year, and still knew so little about Him. A study in contrast they were, with John's fine poet's profile close against grizzle-headed Peter, the bookish eyes of Matthew trading glances with Jesus' kinsman, Jude.

"Truly, I say to you who have followed me in the regeneration, that when the Son of Man shall sit on the throne of majesty, you also shall sit on twelve thrones judging the twelve tribes of Israel.

"And everyone who has left house or brothers or sisters or father or mother or wife or children or lands for My Name's sake shall receive a hundredfold and shall possess life everlasting.

"And many that are first shall be last, and the last shall be first."

Those words of ending seemed lost on the breeze as the Twelve turned to look at each other in that strange mixture of pride and fear that thrills to the promise of great reward.

John bent his head. Nathanael shivered. Judas' eyes gleamed in triumph as unconsciously his hands rubbed against each other.

And Peter looked as if he would like to throw his head back and shout into the wind. Pure delight gripped him. He had left his nets at Jesus' call, with no promise of reward, acting only on his soul's hunger for God. But the sure promise of heaven now was almost more than his giant frame could hold.

Then, like so many other good souls, he had a perfectly human thought. He thought that he should indeed feel sorry for those who did not follow Christ so quickly, and he began to measure the reward which, for instance, the young man could expect against his own. A little surge of pride crossed his chin.

Jesus caught Peter's eye, smiled, and shook His head. And it was then, in that moment of promise, that He told one of the strangest parables of all—the story of the eleventh hour.

He leaned His head back against the knotted olive bark and gently began:

"The kingdom of heaven is like this:

"A rich farmer went out early in the morning to hire laborers to work in his vineyard. And, having agreed with them for a penny a day, he sent them into his vineyard."

The Twelve could see the scene instantly. It was to the bazaar of each town that men went in the morning—the poor seeking work at planting and harvest time, the rich bargaining for good workers. A penny, a denarius, is only about thirty or forty cents in American money, but in those days it bought food for a family. It was a good wage for a full twelve-hour day, from six in the morning to six at night.

Jesus continued. "Then, going out again about the third hour, he saw others standing in the market place idle. And he said to them: 'Go you also into my vineyard and I will give you what shall be just.' And they went their way. And again he went out about the sixth and the ninth hour and did the same."

Matthew's mind still delighted in juggling figures. Three-quarters of a penny the wage should be, he thought, from nine in the morning till six. Half a penny for half a day. A quarter-penny for three hours. Matthew shrugged. What good was three hours' work to either employer or worker? A man would be crazy to go out and hire someone at three in the afternoon!

"But then," said Jesus, "about the eleventh hour he went out and found others standing, and he said to them: 'Why do you stand here all day idle?' And they answered him: 'Because no man has hired us.' And he said to them: 'Go you also into my vineyard.'"

Five o'clock, the eleventh hour of the day! All Twelve grinned at such a notion. A rich man who hired men at the last minute wouldn't stay rich very long, thought Peter. But he had listened carefully, and now, tugging at his short brown beard, he began to think he saw what the parable meant.

We Twelve are like those hired first, he thought. And we will get a full day's wages. While the others will get only—well, "what shall be just." He was already nodding with satisfaction as Jesus continued:

"And when evening came, the lord of the vineyard said to his steward: 'Call the laborers and pay them their wages, beginning with the last even to the first.' And when those who came to work at the eleventh hour came to be paid, each man got a penny."

Peter stopped nodding, his face jolted blank with surprise, as Jesus, eyes twinkling, went on in the same calm voice:

"But when the first came, they thought they should receive more, and yet each of them also received a penny. And they murmured against the master of the house, saying: 'These last have worked only one hour, and you have made them equal to us who have borne the burden and heat of the whole day!'"

He paused, His long strong face turned gently on Peter.

"But the master, answering, said to one of them:

"'Friend, I did you no wrong. Did you not agree with me for a penny? Take what is yours, and go your way. I will also give to this last even as to you. Or is it not lawful for me to do what I will? Do you look for evil in the good that I do?'"

And Jesus stood up firm and tall against the dappled sky. His hands seemed to reach out in dominion over all the spring-green world.

"So shall the last be first, and the first last," said He.

Heaven and earth are Mine, He seemed to say. *And no human mind can fathom or dictate My will. Heaven will be yours if you work for the time I have called you. But I am not injuring you if I give it also to others who seem to you not to have done as much. It is Mine to give—to you and to them. And it is not your task to judge them or to judge Me!*

Even today good men still puzzle the mystery of God's ways, just as the Twelve did then. It still galls some men's pride to see a sinner snatch heaven in a deathbed repentance while we must perhaps trudge through the heat and burden of a whole lifetime to serve God. But pride has no room in heaven. And no mere man can judge what lies behind the late answer of another soul. Indeed some of the last would be first, and the first last—a St. Paul who comes late, as well as a Judas who came soon. In the kingdom there is room for an eleventh-hour soul like the Good Thief as well as for Joseph, who always was just and good.

Peter hitched himself slowly to his feet. Until now he had thought of mercy as a womanish thing, helpless and mild.

Now he saw it instead as the overpowering secret of the almighty God—towering and defeating the mind of man.

Jesus stood, and the Twelve saw in Him the might and justice which went with the traditions of Sinai, steeped in the active justice of the Lord.

But they saw in Him too an incredible loving mercy—the divinely ridiculous loving-kindness of the Savior, surpassing all puny estimates of men.

It is a mystery no man can ever grasp. But it brought the Twelve that day a glimpse of the infinite depths of their God, a glimpse they would never forget.

With a nod Jesus beckoned them back to follow Him on the long road.

And without hesitation Peter fell into step behind Him. He did not even look to see who else walked in those footsteps. He kept his eyes on the Master and followed Him.

34

THE GOOD SHEPHERD*

H<small>E WAS</small> not a man to be intimidated, that was certain. *"Meek,"* He did call Himself, and *"mild." "Gentle Jesus,"* men would call Him in later years.

But it was His audacity that dazzled the eyes of Jerusalem.

He was the most controversial figure of the day. Half the country believed He might well be the Christ. The other half expected His firmly deserved arrest and death at any moment. The city of Jerusalem, her narrow-stepped streets ajostle with pilgrims for the Feast of Tabernacles, bustled with gossip about Him.

The Pharisees were consumed with the urgent desire to destroy Him. Even travelers from the north, come for the feast, knew that. But here, in the bared teeth of danger, this Jesus was teaching openly in the Temple. And what He was saying was either revelation or blasphemy—depending on Who and What He really was.

The bazaars hummed with the latest sayings and doings of Jesus. The inns, the squares where pilgrims camped, were loud with debate.

"Do you know He said today: 'Before Abraham was—*I am!*'"

* John 10:1–18.

"He called Himself the 'Light of the World.' I heard Him."

"He said He was not of this world. And He said if we do not believe that He is the One, we shall die in sin."

And then, on that sabbath, He flaunted His power with an unforgettable miracle, the cure of a man known to be blind since birth. The man was practically a civic landmark. He had been sitting begging outside the Temple for more than twenty years. And Jesus spat on some dirt, made a clay poultice for his eyes, and sent him to wash in the pool of Siloe. The man was healed.

The Pharisees tried desperately to make it out to be a hoax and finally, when the man kept insisting he was cured, when they could see for themselves that his eyes were in fine repair, they threw him bodily out of the Temple.

Jesus found him—Jesus, and His disciples, and the crowd that pressed through the labyrinthine streets below the Temple. And it was there, in front of everyone, that Jesus said to the unblind man:

"Do you believe in the Son of God?"

The man turned newly found sight on Jesus. "Who is He, Lord, that I may believe in Him?"

And Jesus said: "You have seen Him—and it is He Who is talking with you."

The once blind man fell on his knees, his face pressed to the dusty cobbles of the street, to worship Jesus. And he said: "I believe, Lord!"

The Pharisees sneered and gibed in horror. But the crowd listened, and waited.

It was then that Jesus told the parable the world remembers as the tale of the good shepherd—the challenging assertion of His true mission.

They did not understand Him at first. He stood there in the sunset glow of the street, where cold tall angled shadows began to cover the soil and clutter of the city. And He spoke of a sheepfold.

"I say to you that the man who enters not by the door into the sheepfold but climbs up another way is a thief and robber," said Jesus.

And His voice, crisp and calm as a meadow morning, brought with it the sudden picture of a steep wood-fenced pen in the country, nearly square, with one door only, carefully guarded against all danger.

The Pharisees blinked in bewilderment. The crowds, many of them country folk come on foot to the Temple for the holy day, drew closer as men do when caught by nostalgia and the familiar away from home.

"But," said Jesus, "he who enters by the door is the shepherd of the sheep. To him the watchman opens, and the sheep hear his voice, and he calls his own sheep by name and leads them out. And when he has let out his own sheep he goes before them, and the sheep follow him because they know his voice.

"But a stranger they will not follow, but will run away from him because they know not the voice of strangers."

There was a melody to His voice, and men listening in that strange end-of-summer twilight felt a stirring in their hearts, as if in answer to Him. More than one recalled the Psalm of David: *The Lord is my shepherd* . . .

The Pharisees drew a deep breath. They knew, everyone knew, that shepherds were sordid men, beyond the pale of moral and divine respectability. They were under rabbinical ban. Yet this Jesus seemed to enjoy placing peculiar and uncouth emphasis on shepherds in His parables!

Still no one of them, religious expert or homesick farmer, had yet grasped the fullness of the parable. Jesus raised His hand.

"Amen, amen, I say to you—I am the *door* of the sheep.

"And as many as have come before Me are thieves and robbers. And the sheep have not heard them. *I am the door.* If any man enters in by Me, he shall be saved, and shall go in and go out, and shall find pastures.

"The thief comes only to steal and to kill and to destroy. I am come that they may have life, and may have it more abundantly."

Those who came before Me were thieves and robbers? People eyed each other nervously. Perhaps He meant the false Messiahs who had flared for a few months of thunder and then fallen to oblivion? Judas the Galilean had been one. And Theudas another.

For the Pharisees, at least, Jesus made the answer to that unspoken question instantly plain with His next words.

"I am the Good Shepherd," He said.

And as He spoke their Scripture-trained minds flew at once back to the scrolls of the prophets, to what we call the tenth chapter of Isaias, to the twenty-third of Jeremias, but most of all to the Book of Ezekiel: the thirty-eighth chapter of Ezekiel, as we read it now—the terrible warning of God through His prophet some six hundred years before Christ.

There, in verses of branding clarity, God had rebuked the religious leaders of Israel for leading His sheep astray, for not feeding and tending them in the truth, for stealing from them, and abandoning them, while growing fat themselves. And there, in old Scriptures, God had promised that He would rid himself of these shepherds and send a new Shepherd, of the house of David—the Messiah!

"I am the Good Shepherd," said Jesus, His clear dark eyes meeting theirs.

"The Good Shepherd lays down His life for His sheep. But the hireling, the man who is not the shepherd, whose own the sheep are not, sees the wolf coming and leaves the sheep and runs away. The wolf catches and scatters the sheep. And the hireling runs away because he is a hireling and has no care for the sheep."

He lowered His head, the shadows crossing and falling on His brow. And those closest to Him, the Twelve, remembered that He had so often told them in these last days that He would suffer and die. *The Good Shepherd lays down His life* . . .

"I am the Good Shepherd." His voice, stronger now, riding a new current of love, repeated the words of promise. "And I know Mine, and Mine know Me, even as the Father knows Me and I know the Father. And—I lay down My life for My sheep!"

He raised His head, searching the silently growing throng pressed now into doorways and side steps, clogging the street. Gentiles were in that throng, visitors to Jerusalem from all over the Empire. Here and there a Roman face, a Greek, Ethiopian . . .

"And other sheep I have," said Jesus, "that are not of this fold. Them also I must bring, and they shall hear My voice. And there shall be one flock and one Shepherd."

It was a daring statement, imbedded in tones of startling tenderness. You would imagine, thought Peter, that He was actually calling the Gentiles into the kingdom! It was an inconceivable promise, beyond any understanding. Peter shivered. The Pharisees, turning to follow Jesus' glance, seemed to sweep a circle of protection around themselves with the trailing hems of their robes.

Jesus smiled ever so slightly. "Therefore," He said, "the Father loves Me, because I lay down My life that I may take it up again." He flung a sharp glance at His enemies. "No man takes it away from Me. I lay it down of Myself! I have the power to lay it down—and I have the power to take it up again. This is the command I have received from My Father."

For a breath, silence blocked the darkening street. Then Pharisee voices rose in carefully pitched laughter.

"He's possessed by a devil!" they said. "He's mad. Why listen to Him?"

But behind them and around them voices answered:

"Those aren't the words of a man who has a devil."

"Can a devil open the eyes of the blind? He healed this blind man, you know."

In the crackle and prattle of argument Jesus waved a hand in farewell at the man who now could see, and quietly found His way through the crowd and on into the turbulence of Jerusalem at night.

In those few moments He had given the world the parable of His mission on earth and of His Church. Grappling Old Testament and New, prophecy and fulfillment, He had in that tale of the shepherd dying to save his sheep summed up redemption. Freely He would die at the Father's will, to ransom His own.

And who were His own? There would be only one flock drawn from among all men, Gentile and Jew, with one visible head—the Shepherd. The whole flock would He ransom, the whole flock lead and guide in pastures of truth. But each sheep would be known to Him, and each would know Him, alone. And each sheep would come at Jesus' own call, known to Him by name, close in grace, loved and fed and tended by Him.

The words of Ezekiel, the prophet in Babylon, had come true. No longer would the self-centered Pharisees claim to be shepherds. The new Shepherd, a prince of the royal line of David, had come. And from that day on only those who entered in Him could guide His flocks.

All this would eleven of the Twelve remember on that day to come on the shore of Galilee when Jesus, having laid down His life and taken it up again, would say to Peter:

"Feed My sheep. . . .

"Feed My lambs."

Centuries later men would fashion a sweet memory of the Good Shepherd—tender, gentle, sweet-faced. But those who heard Him that evening in Jerusalem knew that He was also flamboyant and daring, firm as a countryman armed against the beasts.

35

THE TWO SONS*

H<small>E WAS</small> not interested in what men said.

It seemed at times as if he barely listened—or perhaps as though He had been listening for so incredibly long a time to the mouthings of piety that His ears were tired. He had a habit of looking into the lines of your face, into the light of your eyes, as if reading the hidden history of your life. You had to look away or forget what you were saying. . . .

You could not lie to Him. Men had tried. He could detect shame as other men detect the stench of garbage. And it was in dealing with hypocrites that He won a strange reputation as a master of invective and insult.

He was the essence of truth. And truth, complete and living truth, is an exhausting thing, a burden too heavy for most men to carry. They could go a little of the road with Him, but as He Himself said it was a narrow and difficult path. If He had been willing to compromise, if He had diluted His doctrines, or been willing to overlook a little foot-dragging, He could have drawn an army of disciples. As it was, He lost a great many who could not pretend to be what they were not. Reluctantly, they left Him.

He did seem to understand, which was a comfort. He

* Matthew 21:28–32.

would watch them leave and say nothing in rebuke. It was, oddly enough, almost as if He honored them for their honesty in stepping back.

You could not help loving a Man like that, even after you left Him.

And yet it was hard to understand why He should slash with such whiplike scorn at the Pharisees and say nothing to the fallen-away people of the streets. The Pharisees had their faults, but at least they were openly dedicated to God, men with their feet on the ladder to heaven. It seemed it would be kinder and more constructive of Jesus to encourage them and lead them upward, instead of making them His enemies.

But the knife of a surgeon is not always polite.

His attack on the Pharisees and Scribes, on all the fusty Temple aristocracy, was the talk of Israel. His words were quoted and savored in the fountain-cooled dining halls of the rich Romans and the tiny houses of the poor alike.

He said the Pharisees were like hidden graves, over which people walked innocently, thinking them good ground.

He said they were whitewashed tombs—pretty as a monument outside, hideous with bones and worms inside.

He called them snakes and vipers and hypocrites and sons of hell.

He ridiculed them for overdressing the role of piety, for wearing their prescribed tassels so long they needed combing, for traipsing around giving alms and saying prayers where they were sure of an audience. He accused them of a double standard of piety, of burdening common folk with their ironbound interpretations of Scripture while they found convenient loopholes in the commandments for themselves.

There was nothing personal in His abuse. He hated not the sinner but the sin, not the Pharisee or the code he taught but the calculated straddling of the spiritual fence.

He had told the crowd: "The Scribes and the Pharisees have been seated on the chair of Moses. All the things that they say to you, therefore, observe and do. But do not act according to the way they act—for they say one thing and do another!"

In public the Pharisees laughed and pretended that what He said would not be taken seriously by anyone. Privately they called Him a clever exhibitionist and a rabble-rouser, capitalizing on the envy and hatred of the cursed multitudes, which was their way of speaking of the less righteous common folk.

"He makes friends with sinners and insults the good," they said to the people. "All around Him are harlots and drunkards and thieves—and who has heard Him speak harshly to them? A fine kind of prophet He is, pampering those who offend God and attacking His servants in the Temple! *He* is the real hypocrite!"

Even the multitudes, cursed or not, found it confusing. What He said about the Pharisees was true, they knew. But what they said about Him seemed true too.

What *is* truth? Are there different kinds of truth, two ways and more of judging?

He answered that question one day in the Temple, when He told the parable of the two sons.

He had come there to teach. It was the day after His fantastic entry into Jerusalem, when the crowds had swarmed in an extravagant spontaneous welcome fit only for a king. He had ridden then in triumph to the Temple, while they trooped after Him singing His praises and calling Him the promised "Son of David."

This morning there were no triumphal processions. But there were still crowds. He had caused a small riot already by wrecking the booths of the sheep and dove sellers and whipping the slippery-fingered money-changers. He had called the Temple His "Father's House," and He drove them out of it. . . .

People jostled each other in the long outer corridor of the Temple to see and hear Him.

When the Temple dignitaries, the priests and the Scribes and the Pharisees, strode out to challenge Him, everyone held his breath. The skirmish at first was quiet, an exchange of question answered by question in the typical manner of Jewish conversation. They asked for His credentials. He countered with an inquiry about John the Baptist.

The people could not hear too well. They fidgeted, feeling the tension grow, seeing nothing happen. But Jesus never dallied with formalities. He moved directly to the heart of the matter.

When He told that parable everyone there could hear Him.

"A certain man," He began—and those who were not strangers to Jerusalem felt the welcome familiarity of those opening words.

"A certain man had two sons. And, coming to the first, he said:

" 'Son, go work today in my vineyard.'

"And he, answering, said: 'I will not.'

"But afterward, being moved with repentance, he went."

The men of Jerusalem, the pilgrims from Galilee and Judea and Perea, from outpost colonies of Jewish faith all over the Empire, smiled. There was human nature for you—the young man who growls and rebels and regrets and obeys. They had done it themselves. Their own sons did the same.

Jesus continued: "And, coming to the other son, he said the same thing. And that son, answering, said:

" 'I go, sir!'

"And he did not go."

The men grinned. There was always a son like that too, the kind the world thought was perfect—so amiable, such a willing lad! At times such a one could fool even himself. . . .

Jesus turned and held a question out to the Pharisees and the priests. "Which of the two did the father's will?"

The Pharisees, lowering their eyelids in ill-concealed impatience, said: "The first, of course."

Jesus nodded and folded His hands in front of Him, as if in meditation. "Amen, I say to you that the publicans and the harlots will go into the kingdom of God before you."

The words lay like a line of battle drawn in the heavy air.

"For John came to you," He said, "in the way of justice, and you did not believe him. The publicans and the harlots believed him. But you, seeing it, did not even repent afterward, that you might believe him."

Understanding ran like a murmur through that throng, passing in suddenly widened eyes, in elbow nudges, in humming breaths.

One man says he will not go and he goes. Another says he will go and does not go. And there before you is the problem of truth—of lip service and action, of hypocrisy and honesty.

The sinners, at least, did not pretend to be holy. They were honest in their rebellion—truthful before God and men and themselves. And in time the honesty of their hearts would drive them to change their minds and go.

But the Pharisees had convinced even themselves that they were obedient sons. They had said a hundred times a day to the Lord: "I go, sir!" And they did not go. They did not obey the will of God. And they expected the world to give them credit for their words, while they took their comfort in avoiding the harsher edges of action. . . .

Truth is in a man's action and his will—not in his words alone, Jesus was saying. There is greater truth in the open sinner who admits he is too weak to leave his sin than in the pious gentry of faith too weak to confess they dare not practice what they preach.

Jesus listened not to words but to hearts. He knew the way of God's sons—recognized the last burst of rebellion in one, the oily evasion of another.

Within three days Jesus Himself would stand for judgment, and to Pilate He would say:

"Everyone that is of the truth hears My voice."

And Pilate would ask:

"What is truth?"

Jesus would answer not a word. He was doing the will of His Father, then and always. He was the truth.

36

THE TENANT FARMERS*

HE WAS not, by anyone's standards, handsome. He was tall, perhaps a good six inches more than most men, well formed and straight. But the face was plain, almost homely.

A man, to capture public fancy, has usually a certain animal magnetism, a red cheek, a flashing eye, an air of expert grooming or a certain deliberately careless charm. He had neither.

He simply—*was*. No other word would do.

And yet He held the people in His hand. They loved Him as if He were their father, their brother, the one who held the key to their inner yearning.

It was very difficult for a casual onlooker to understand.

He stood in the Temple teaching, speaking quietly to about a hundred people gathered into an antechamber. Only yesterday He had ridden into Jerusalem as if He were a king, a triumphant entry with crowds singing and strewing His way with their cloaks and with palm branches. The Temple seemed still to echo the children's hosannas.

Then the chief priests had come to Him in indignation. He had answered them calmly, and in His own good time He had left.

* Matthew 21:33–45; Mark 12:1–9; Luke 20:1–19.

Yet here He was back today. *His Father's House,* He had called this Temple when He whipped the animal salesmen and kicked over the tables of the money-changers. And He still looked as if He owned the place.

Not that He was insolent. Even the chief priests, watching Him, had to admit there was no bravado about Him, no swagger to His stance. He was not, they knew, the kind of upstart you could hustle off into any alley and be rid of. He had invaded their domain and He seemed convinced of victory. He was busy, teaching, apparently not caring in the least about chief priests or elders or Scribes or Pharisees.

And they did not know what to do about Him. They were, after all, the acknowledged public authorities on God. Everyone in Israel knew that they were His chosen chief servants, guarding His revelations and truth. They themselves were quite aware of their importance, even if this Jesus was not.

And they were faced here with a Person who in this very Temple had let children salute Him as the Messiah, the Christ.

Others before Jesus had claimed to be the Christ. But none of them had been quite as difficult to handle. This fellow did not seem mad, as they did. He had an admirable knowledge of Scripture, and He could hold His own in any argument. But there was something else about Him too.

He behaved, as one of the elders had said in strictest privacy, as if He were a prince in disguise—a man with a tremendous secret, to the purple bred, as you might say. And that was a most unsettling thought.

They came, a delegation of the chief priests and elders, to challenge Him that morning. The crowd parted for them. And Jesus, finishing what He was saying, turned to greet them in silence.

"What authority have You to do these things?" The voice

of an elder clattered across the room like a dropped sword. "And who gave You that authority?"

He bent His head. His eyebrows raised a trifle as He parried their questions.

"Let Me ask you one question," He said. "Answer it, and I will tell you by Whose authority I act. Tell Me—where did John the Baptist get the authority to baptize, from heaven or from men?"

The chief priests whispered to the elders. The elders whispered to each other. "If we say, 'From heaven,' He will ask us why we did not believe John. But if we say, 'From men,' the crowds will give us trouble, for they believe John was a prophet."

There was only one safe answer.

"We do not know!" they said to Jesus, and their tone tried to imply that after all the question was unimportant and quite irrelevant.

He shrugged. "Neither will I tell you by what authority I act. But"—He raised His head and held them pinioned with His glance—"what do you think of this?"

And then, to the delight of the people whom He had been teaching, He began to tell a parable designed especially for the priests and the elders.

"There was a man," He said, "who planted a vineyard."

He paused. Each word seemed chiseled in the air, deceptively simple. Yet His eyes seemed to press on the priests and elders with strange urgency.

"And he planted a hedge around it and dug a wine press in it. And he built a tower."

They knew their Scripture, these priests and elders. They knew the Book of Isaias the prophet by heart, the same verses that we find in our Bibles in the fifth chapter of that book.

There too someone had planted a vineyard, and fenced it in, and built a wine press and a tower.

"For the vineyard of the Lord of hosts is the house of Israel," Isaias had said. And the One who planted it is God.

Jesus nodded as the first flash of understanding crossed their faces. And He went on:

"And the man leased his vineyard to some tenant farmers and went away to a distant country. And when the harvest time came he sent his servants to the farmers to collect the fruit from his vineyard. And the farmers, seizing his servants, beat one and killed one and stoned another.

"And again he sent other servants to the vineyard, more men than before. And they treated those servants the same way."

He stopped, His voice seeming to falter under an invisible weight. But His head was high and His gaze did not waver.

"And last of all," said Jesus, "he sent to them his son, saying: 'At least they will honor my son.'

"But the farmers, seeing the son, said among themselves: 'This is the heir! Come, let us kill him, and then we shall have his inheritance.'

"And, taking him, they threw him out of the vineyard and killed him."

The room was utterly silent. From the distance the echo of footsteps sounded, the everyday noises of men and women coming to offer sacrifice and prayer, the singing and praying and coughing of a routine morning. But in this antechamber no one moved.

Then Jesus turned to the delegation.

"Tell Me, when the owner of the vineyard shall come himself, what will he do to those farmers?"

One of the elders cleared his throat and sniffed. "He will bring those evil men to an evil end," he said solemnly. "And he will of course rent his vineyard to other farmers who will give him his harvest at the proper time."

Jesus nodded.

"Therefore, I say to you that the kingdom of God shall be taken from you—and given to a nation that will give the Lord harvest."

They had asked for a statement. They had one.

There was no doubting His meaning. The vineyard was God's, and it had been given to the care of the priests of Israel. The servants God sent were the prophets—who had indeed been stoned and beaten and killed in the past. And the Pharisees, like the tenant farmers of the parable, had grown heady with power and greedy, serving their own interests rather than God's.

Then God, being infinitely patient, had sent His Son. And that Son would be killed because He by His rights threatened the power of the chief priests.

And the priests would lose their power. And God would give the vineyard to another nation for the harvest.

Jesus stood before them. He had, in so many words, called Himself the Son of God. And no one dared protest. The chief priests and Pharisees knew precisely what He was saying. He was insisting that no one confuse Him with one of God's servants. He was the Son.

Their hands itched to seize Him then and there, just as the farmers had seized the heir. But they were afraid—not of Jesus, not of God, but of the people.

The disciples, who sat among the crowd, were pale as they grappled with the meaning of that parable. Not yet could they fully realize the role they would play in its ending, realize that they were to be the new caretakers of God's vineyard, replacements for those same priests and elders who stood now in anger in the Temple. And their fate would be little easier than that of the servants of the past, the prophets. Like them, they would die serving the Lord of the vineyard.

They were, all Twelve, as Jesus Himself was, born Jews— proud of the heritage of Israel. They knew that God had chosen Israel as His own and planted His vine in this vineyard. They would remember it when Christ would say to them only a few days from this: "I am the Vine, and you are the branches."

And they would find to their own heartache that the harvest from the Vine would be yielded by a new chosen people. And as the first years of Christianity passed they would understand that the parable of the tenant farmers was perfect prophecy.

But they would see in it another meaning too. For, like all His parables, it is a story not of one time alone but of eternal truth.

The wicked tenant farmers did not die with the Pharisees. The world is still filled with self-righteous people who have no intention of letting God get in their way. Like the men of the parable, they refuse to give God the harvest.

They forget that nothing here is ours, after all. Whether material riches or treasures of the spirit, they belong to God and we hold them only in trust. He may strip from us the little money we have; it is not ours. He may take away our health, our families, our friends. They are not ours. We are, all of us, tenant farmers in this world. And as the harvest passes through our hands we must be content with the share due us for our work.

And when He sends His servants to us we must greet them honestly and in obedience. For they, and His Son, will come to each of us too. They come in strange guises, these messengers and the Son. Yet only pride can keep us from seeing them—pride and the odd belief that refusal to heed them makes lords of us.

The farmers who murdered the son did not get to keep his inheritance.

Nor did those conspirators who watched the Son stride through the Temple that day begin to know what His murder would mean—for them, or for us.

37

THE FIG TREE BRANCHES*

THERE was always a sense of mystery about Him, a depth
that defied the soundings of human understanding.

Of all His friends not one could claim to know Him completely. When He was a child, even His mother did not always understand what He did. As a man, he embarrassed
many of His relatives in Nazareth. The two who did join Him
as disciples, James and Jude, were still slow to catch His
meaning.

Little things He did and said—the way He behaved the
night Martha was cooking dinner, His delay when Lazarus
sickened, His sudden destruction of a fruitless but innocent
fig tree—baffled those who loved Him most.

He took pains to spell out the truth that impelled Him
through life and death, but the truth was too great for His
followers to absorb. He told the Twelve again and again the
details of His coming sufferings. He said He would be mocked
and scourged and condemned and crucified. He said He
would die. And that He would rise again from death. But
when He was arrested they fell to pieces with disillusion and
fear.

Even when they knew Him risen from death, even in the

* Matthew 24:32–33; Luke 21:29–31.

glory of resurrection, they did not understand. If He could break the chains of death and live again, He could have avoided death in the first place. Why would He allow Himself to die?

They were not yet completely naturalized citizens of heaven. They still thought in the old patterns. The language and customs of the world clung to them.

Only with time, and the intimate forceful presence of the Holy Spirit, would they understand the meaning of His sacrifice. Without God's help no man can understand God—even when He speaks.

They had thought of Jesus as primarily a teacher—a rabbi, a prophet, a master to guide men to knowledge of heaven. But Jesus had come not to teach—but to *be*. He came to become man and to redeem man. He spoke of God, and testified to Him, and described life with Him—much the way any son will speak of his father, lovingly, reverently, constantly. But at the last meal He ate on earth, the first holy communion, when He made His farewells to the Twelve, Jesus gave them a promise:

"The Advocate, the Holy Spirit, Whom the Father will send in My name—*He* will teach you all things."

And Jesus, the Son of God and of Man, the Redeemer, went His way to Gethsemane and to the Cross.

He had spoken as much as He could, as much as their minds could hold of the infinite vibrant truth of heaven and earth. He had clothed the truth in human words and linked it to the life they knew.

But there were some truths that could not be made clear, some that were to remain mysteries. And such was the truth of the tale of the fig tree and its branches—the parable no one understood.

They had asked Him:

"What will be the signs of Your coming—and of the end of the world?"

They had felt all that day, in fact ever since the morning when He rode over the palm branches, as if thunder brewed in the distance. The air was still and shiny, breathless before some unseen turmoil to fall. Doom echoed in their ears, and they shied at shadows.

He had spoken again of His death. He had prophesied the destruction of the beautiful Temple, there in the city below His seat under the trees of Mount Olivet. He had said, too, that at the end of the world He would return in glory to judge the living and the dead.

"When will these things be?" they asked. And even as they asked they were not sure of what they meant—the end of Jerusalem? the time He would come again? the last day of earth?

His tall lean body, still young and strong in His thirty-third year, stood profiled against the smoldering clouds of twilight. The olive trees, old and bearded, loomed like a black frame around Him. In the distance the great and holy Temple of Jerusalem looked unreal as a castle in the sand.

And He spoke then as never before, in a kind of reverie—as if all of time were spread before Him, twisted and tormented as it reached upward to His outstretched hand.

Watching Him, the Twelve felt that His fingers could have held the whole future, so small did it seem beside Him. It was not time that bulked large in His eyes but the anguish and the hope, the beauty and the terror of the strife of heaven and hell. Just as a man looking down at the city could not force himself to see the orange peel on the bazaar street, or the child laughing near the Sheep Gate—so Jesus seemed as He looked at the future to see only the peaks and turrets against the sky.

He knew when a sparrow fell from the air, knew the paths of men and nations through all the centuries. But it would take more than all of time to describe the many faces of the road ahead.

He was not their soothsayer. He was their Christ, come to save them, to lift them up with Him. And when He spoke it was in words of warning.

" . . . wars and rumors of wars . . ." He said. " . . . pestilences and famines and earthquakes . . . But all these things are only the beginning of sorrows. . . ." Persecution and death. Betrayal and hatred. False prophets. All these He saw like reefs in the water, like snares on the path.

He paused, and saw His disciples straining to mark each sign in their memories, and smiled. The end of the world?

"The gospel of the kingdom shall be preached in the whole world, for a testimony to all nations, and *then* shall the end come."

His eyes turned back to Jerusalem, and tears rose in His throat. The holy city would be dashed to ruin, destroyed till not a stone lay on another. It would be the "abomination of desolation" of which Daniel the prophet spoke, a time of vengeance and horror. . . .

His voice rode on through the evening, searching the future, lighting in warning, then taking up its journey again toward the end of time. There would be false Christs, and wonders and signs to deceive even those who love God. They must not be led astray. There would be no mistaking the true Second Coming. When He returned it would not be as a Baby hidden in a stable. Not as a Carpenter in a tiny corner of earth.

"For as lightning comes out of the east and appears even to the west, so shall also the coming of the Son of Man be."

He flung His head back to rest on the gnarled olive tree.

"But immediately after the tribulation of those days the sun shall be darkened, and the moon shall not give her light, and the stars shall fall from heaven, and the powers of heaven shall be moved. And *then* shall appear the sign of the Son of Man in heaven.

"And then shall the tribes of the earth mourn, and they shall see the Son of Man coming in the clouds of heaven with power and majesty. And He shall send His angels with a trumpet and a great voice. And they shall gather together His elect from the four winds, from the furthest parts of the heavens to the utmost bounds of them."

The Twelve sat like children rapt in the spell of a story they could not quite understand. He turned in the growing darkness and said:

"Now from the fig tree learn a parable. When its branch is now tender and the leaves come forth, you know that summer is near.

"So you also, when you shall see all these things, know that it is near, even at the doors.

"Amen, I say to you that this generation shall not pass until all these things be done. Heaven and earth shall pass away, but My words shall not pass."

They grasped at that parable as a man in a foreign country snatches at the one phrase of the language he knows. A fig tree in springtime. Every one of them knew what it was to run his hand over a branch of a fig—so stiff in the winter's sleep, so suddenly supple in the warmth of growth. The leaves burst from that tender branch, yellow-green in the first unfurling of life.

Anyone could recognize a fig tree's announcement of spring. Then surely anyone could recognize the signs He had foretold?

From that night till now men have argued the meaning of

His prophecies. There were days when His followers believed that the destruction of Jerusalem, which did come in the year A.D. 70, did mean the end of the world—that the Second Coming would follow as quickly as the bud and leaf of a wakening tree. Jerusalem was trampled to the ground, and the world went on.

There were years when the first Christians waited daily for the end of the world, postponing business and pleasure so as to be ready.

Signs came and went. Before the fall of Jerusalem there were earthquakes and disasters. There still are today. Wars and persecutions have peppered the centuries. False prophets have walked the streets. And still the world endures.

There are some who believe the "generation that will not pass away" meant the people of Israel, some who believe it meant the Christian era. Those who thought it meant the contemporaries of Jesus have died and gone themselves.

There are men who believe the end of the world of which He spoke is coming within our own lifetime. And others say that He spoke only of the private personal end of the world for each man—that each life would contain wars and calamities and temptations against faith. . . .

"From the fig tree learn a parable," He said.

Nearly two thousand springs have softened the branches of fig trees, and the parable is not yet learned. The future is as much a mystery as ever.

But there are those who watch the drama of spring, see the branch bend and swell and leaf, and feel that He meant us to find in each spring new warning, a new awareness that at any hour the soul must be ready.

"The signs will be clear," He said. And He meant for us to watch for them. "Watch the fig tree," He said. And the signs of spring come again and again, in the circle of the years.

"Take heed! Watch! Be ready! For you know not the hour. . . ."

The echoes of His voice are in the heralds of each new year.

He had not made Himself clear as men would want. He did not intend to. He came to live and die and to rise again, to share His life with all who would be born again in Him. He was a Man among men. He was also the Son of God. The future is hidden still in God. And it can be understood only by life in Him.

In the garden the chill wind of the spring night moved through the olive branches. The signs of summer were not there.

38

THE TEN VIRGINS*

H E DID not own that spot on the hillside, not by the law
of property and of deed. But He had made it His, claimed it
with the innocent ease of one at home on God's earth. As a
child may make an apple-tree branch his heart's home, as a
woman may walk through the tall shore grass to a single
boulder to dream, or a man seek one river pool, so Jesus went
to the garden with the olive press on the hill.

The olive trees, gray-green as a whisper, stood in wind-
rustle over the deep damp green of the grass. Below lay the
brook of Kedron, a wild torrent in the spring rains, and beyond it the massive shape of the Temple. Jerusalem, her walls
wrapped in mist, looked legendary in her loveliness from this
height. The garden was a retreat from the brattle and rush
of the city, a place where a man could breathe and look at
the sky.

It was not that He held Himself aloof from the crowds or
the business of living. He was no hermit. He could not afford
the luxury of solitude. Day after grueling day He spent Himself in the throngs of towns, refusing no one. His pace tired
even Matthew, the one city-bred fellow of the Twelve.

But, as a man must sleep to live, so he must also have quiet

* Matthew 25:1–13.

for the spirit or die of exhaustion. And in this last week before Passover, with the shouts of the palm procession still
reverberating through Jerusalem, with the arguments of the
Pharisees clattering in the Temple, Jesus climbed the slope to
Gethsemane.

He had the ability to rest completely and immediately
whenever and wherever there was time. As simply as an in-
fant He could shed the pressure of the day and lie back as if
in His Father's arms. And yet, the disciples well knew, He
was always alert. It was as if at any moment a call might
come, and He would rise to meet it. It was an ability they
did not share.

The Twelve turned to look down at Jerusalem stretched out
in the haze. And they called to Jesus to come and see the
Temple buildings like a child's sand castle below them. They
were, after all, still sight-seers in the great city, tourists in
their spare time. And they had not had their fill of Jerusalem's
wonders.

He did not move from where He lay under the trees. He
simply said:

"Do you see all these things? Indeed, I tell you there shall
not be left one stone on a stone that shall not be destroyed!"

They were not prepared for such a voice of doom. The rain
had cleared. The touch of spring was in the breeze. It was
too sweet an afternoon to think of the coming of the end of
the world or of Jerusalem. And yet—that was what Jesus was
thinking of. And the urgency in His voice drew them to His
side.

They asked Him, as they had so often before:

"Tell us, when shall these things come to be? And what
will be the sign of Your coming and of the consummation of
the world?"

It was a question without an answer. Three questions in one, really.

As they were one day to understand, He spoke to them of three separate events which they could not quite distinguish in their minds. He spoke of the destruction of Jerusalem—a prophecy which would come devastatingly true within the next forty years. He spoke also of the last day, when the whole world would end. In that final day He, the Son of Man and Son of God, would come in an earth-shattering glory of justice, and the stars and the heavens would be in torment and turmoil.

And He spoke also of the last day of earthly life for each separate soul—of the day when He would come to call each one individually to judgment and reckoning.

"But," said Jesus, "of that day and hour no one knows—not even the angels of heaven, but the Father alone."

And He said: "Therefore you must be ready, because you do not know at what hour the Son of Man will come."

He leaned forward, His fingers twined in the long grass, the thin olive leaves arching over His head. And He told them then the parable of the ten virgins.

"Then," He said, "the kingdom of heaven shall be like this:

"There were ten virgins who, taking their lamps, went out to meet the bridegroom and the bride."

Some of the Twelve looked down at the Temple, and they remembered the Pharisees' anger at the way Jesus spoke so often in parables of weddings and marriage feasts. The Pharisees thought Him blasphemous, for as all good Jews knew God Himself spoke of the end of the world and of heaven as the great marriage feast.

"And five of them," said Jesus, "were foolish. And five were wise.

"The five foolish women, having taken their lamps, did not

take oil with them. But the wise took oil in small jars with their lamps.

"And the bridegroom tarried so long that they all slumbered and slept."

He smiled, with disarming gentleness, and they could almost see the ten earnest young women, all decked in their finery, snoring away like children at the bend of the road before the bridegroom's house.

"And at midnight," said Jesus, "a cry went up: 'See, the bridegroom comes! Go and meet him!'

"Then all these young virgins got up and began to trim their lamps. And the foolish said to the wise ones: 'Give us some of your oil, for our lamps have gone out!'

"The wise answered: 'Perhaps there might not be enough for us and for you. You had better go to the oil sellers and buy some for yourselves.'"

Buy oil in the middle of the night? The Twelve could practically hear the twitter and prattle of the women, fussing and scrambling to be ready for the big moment.

"Now while they went to buy oil," said Jesus, "the bridegroom came. And the ones who were ready went in with him to the wedding. And the door was shut.

"But at last the other virgins came also, saying: 'Lord! Lord! Open to us!'

"But he answered: 'Indeed, I say to you—I know you not!'"

Jesus stood, His head bent over the Twelve, His voice grave.

"Watch therefore—because you do not know the day or the hour!"

And He strode over the green to the crest of the hill, looking down on the city He loved.

The bridegroom would not come on schedule, that was plain. He would tarry so long that all excitement would wither, and even the best of souls would grow drowsy and sleep. There had been no reproach for the women for sleeping at their posts. Indeed, thought Peter, it's as if He were answering our question by telling us that the end will not come till we are almost beyond waiting for it—centuries from now, perhaps thousands of years.

But when He does come the soul must be ready. There will be no time to scurry about and make provision. No one can give us the grace we shall need then. The door will be closed, and the Lord will not open it again. There is, thought Peter, not one moment when it will be safe to take a vacation from holiness!

Through the years men have pondered that parable—through the first years of Christianity when people expected the world to end any moment, on to today when some people seem to think it will never end while others eye each new bomb with terror.

We have no such marriage feasts now, no procession of virgins to welcome the groom and bride to his house. We do not use oil lamps except perhaps on camping expeditions. We think of preparedness in terms of war, not of feasting.

Perhaps, if He were to tell the parable today, He might frame it in terms of preparation for invasion or disaster. But there were wars facing Palestine then, and he did not choose war for an example. The end of the world to the Christian is not a disaster or an emergency. It is the supreme opening of happiness and rejoicing.

He might remind us of children waiting to greet their father on his return from a long journey, falling asleep with their bouquets wilting in their hands. Or of a young man waiting for the one chance of his career, the understudy waiting to be called and forgetting to study her lines. Or of a woman keeping a candle lit in a window as a sign for a man long overdue, letting the flame die on the one night he would pass by.

The chance of a lifetime, we say. And in each of our lives there will be the one last day and hour when He comes to us.

"Watch, for you know not the day or the hour!"

Jesus rested in the garden under the trees, His eyes closing with the sweep and dance of the leaves in the wind. He knew the day and the hour.

39

THE WEDDING GARMENT*

HE STOOD in the stormlight of the afternoon as it filtered through the Temple windows. He spoke so quietly that His listeners had to strain forward, bearded chins resting on their knees. And yet that voice struck like lightning into the secret recesses of each man's heart.

Some there were among the elders and the Pharisees, in their glittering robes and phylacteries, who remembered a time more than twenty years before when a Boy had stood where He stood now, a stripling of twelve. The Boy had borne Himself with courtesy and gentle manners as He did now. Hour after hour the lad had discussed the Law with the best religious minds in the Temple, not asking but teaching with a wisdom that clashed with His young brown curls and bare feet.

That had been, they thought then, the debate of the century, an unforgettable drama ended only by a pair of weeping parents come to fetch the Boy.

And those who remembered could trace the same voice, the same bearing in the Man whom some called Master and others Christ. The debate had not ended. It had only been interrupted.

* Matthew 22:1–14.

He still spoke with a maddening mixture of courtesy and authority—so mildly that you could not accuse Him of insolence or bravado, so firmly that you knew He would accept no challenge.

On one side of the Temple antechamber sat His twelve disciples and an equally motley assortment of men who were nobodies—pilgrims, some of them, come for Passover. On the other side stood the men who mattered in the Temple—the priests, the Pharisees, the elders.

And in the center Jesus—lean, strong, dramatic only in His utter plainness and in the breath of clean freshness that seemed to surround Him. It was as if He brought with Him into the smoky traffic-filled Temple the world of the sea and the field. And He stood not with the careful refinement of a Pharisee but with the self-contained dignity of a man alone with God's wind and rain.

He had already so angered the Pharisees that they itched to lay hold of Him and destroy Him. He had told them plainly that they did not have either goodness or sense to recognize Him for what He was. He had announced that they were not the holy souls they thought themselves to be. And He had said that God was most displeased with them, and that they would come to an evil end.

They did not dare do anything to Him then and there, because the people, who did not know any better, did believe He was at least a prophet, if not the actual Messiah. There was nothing the Pharisees could do but listen and bide their time.

The plain people, the nobodies, on the other hand were fascinated. They did believe that Jesus came from God and that He spoke divine truth. And to their surprise His truth and the Pharisees' were utterly different.

The Pharisees had made it plain that God and heaven were

their private property. The Jews as a whole were the chosen people. But the Pharisees were the chosen ones among them!

But Jesus said:

"The kingdom of heaven is like this:

"A king made a marriage feast for his son."

The Pharisees grunted. Any fool who studied Scripture could understand that. The prophets were always comparing the relation between God and His people to a marriage, and the final union with Him in heaven to a great wedding feast. The reference to the king's son, however, was disturbing. This Jesus was always speaking of the Son of God—and of the Son of Man.

"And he sent his servants," said Jesus quietly, "to call those invited to come to the feast. But they would not come.

"Again he sent out other servants, saying: 'Tell those who are invited I have prepared my dinner, my oxen and calves are killed, and everything is ready. Come to the marriage feast!'"

Jesus faced the Pharisees, His face gray in the sober storm-light. "But they did not take it seriously, and they went their ways, one to his farm, another to his business. And the rest of them laid hold of his servants, and insulted them, and then put them to death."

The Pharisees raised polite eyebrows.

"But when the king heard that," said Jesus, "he was angry. And he sent his armies, destroyed the murderers, and burned their city.

"Then he said to his servants: 'The marriage feast is ready, but those who were invited were not worthy. Go out then to the crossroads and invite whomever you find.' And his servants went out into the highways and gathered all they found, both good and bad. And the marriage feast was filled with guests."

His disciples, the Twelve gathered in a gloomy corner of the room, smiled at each other. They had, they thought, heard this parable before—about the great supper. God was the king. And the Jews, the Pharisees in particular, were those invited. They had been invited, you might say, back in the days of Abraham. And the first set of servants were the prophets, who were not taken very seriously at all. And the second set were perhaps themselves, these Twelve, and Jesus Himself.

The Twelve looked at the Pharisees and tried not to grin at their discomfiture. How it would disturb the proper ones to see heaven overrun with a bunch of nobodies!

The nobodies themselves leaned forward with a smug look. This Master made the kingdom of heaven seem most wonderfully easy to enter. All you had to do was come when you were called!

But this was not quite the same parable. And the ending was not so simple.

"Now," said Jesus, turning His attention to the disciples and the others, His back to the Pharisees. "The king went in to see the guests. And he saw there a man who did not have on a wedding garment."

That was, even the most uncouth man knew, the peak of rudeness. You did not have to go out and buy clothes for the feast. The bridegroom's family provided the garment. All you had to do was pick it up and put it on. There was no excuse not to wear it.

"And he said to him: 'Friend, how did you come here without a wedding garment?' But the man was silent. Then the king said to his servants: 'Tie his hands and feet and throw him into the outer darkness, where there will be weeping and gnashing of teeth.'

"For many are called, but few are chosen."

Far off over the hills below the city, near the valley called Gehenna, the storm began and it could be heard even here in the busy Temple. Gehenna—the place where evil smoldering fires smoked day and night, consuming the rubbish of Jerusalem! It had become the name and symbol of damnation for the Jews, the place of outer darkness and eternal pain.

The Twelve, and the pilgrims crowded near them, felt a shiver pass down their souls like the fingers of rain.

Even though God threw open the gates of His kingdom to all, though He called the sinner as well as the Pharisee, He would not save a soul by the scruff of its neck, thought Andrew. There was no room for carelessness or evil in heaven. Without a proper dress, without being cleaned up, no one was coming to stay in the kingdom. That was obvious. If you made no effort to be worthy of the great honor of being called, you were sentenced with no possible escape, bound hand and foot.

In a way, thought Andrew, the Pharisees who refused to come were more honest—and better off—than those who came unprepared.

In the gathering darkness Jesus smiled, His arms spread in silent invitation. And to those who listened and watched, it seemed that a man would be a fool to be called into the kingdom and come without the wedding garment of holiness and grace that Christ offered him.

In the years ahead His servants would carry the call to the kingdom of heaven to all men everywhere, to you and to me. No one in the world would be left off the list. But not everyone would be there at that nuptial feast of the Son. Some have refused. Some have indeed persecuted and murdered His messengers.

And some of us have accepted and then appreciated the honor so little that we have come in our old clothes, grimed and stained, out at the elbow. There are some who think the invitation is a guarantee, a carte blanche to trust God's goodness and slop about as they please. They will not stay long at the feast. The King may come at any moment. And the fires still smolder in the outer darkness.

It all comes down, thought Andrew, to this idea that men get about being the chosen people. The Pharisees were so sure that they had been chosen that they began to think the Lord ought to be grateful to them for coming. And they had become un-chosen.

But the same goes for us, Andrew nodded. We have been called. And we're likely to get quite cocksure of ourselves because of it. The Pharisees are not the only snobs in the world.

He looked at the Master with a prayer in his heart that the meekness of the Christ would remain with him and all who are called forever.

"Many are called, but few are chosen."

He spoke softly, but the words echoed through the vaulted corridors of the Temple in the effable sadness of the loving God.

40

THE TRUE VINE[*]

It was His farewell dinner.

He was leaving them, and they refused to understand that He had told them how and why and where He would go. They knew only that this year's Passover feast, the fourth they had eaten with Him, was like no other. And the tide of love that swelled in their souls was beyond all speaking.

They felt on the verge of a mystery of life, as if each word and action of His curtained the entrance of a new world.

There had been the moment when He said over the bread: "This is My Body,"

when He said over the wine:

"This is My Blood,"

and had given to them to eat and to drink.

And because it was Passover, the feast that recalled the ransom of Israel from bondage in Egypt, meaning and symbol were in the air, till the history of the past seemed mingled with the present to become a new truth. The blood of a lamb on a doorpost had been the sign that preserved the children of Israel from death that night in Egypt. And here was Blood, the Blood of the One John the Baptist called the Lamb of God. . . .

[*] John 15:1-9.

Jesus said: "This is My Blood of the new testament, which shall be shed for many unto the remission of sins."

And they remembered the day when He had told the world that unless a man eat His flesh and drink His blood he would not have life in him. He had scandalized many that day, and they had turned and left Him. He could have called them back and said they misunderstood. But He had not done so. He had meant precisely what He said.

The disciples had so many questions to ask Him this night. The urgency of parting was on them, and they knew they had not yet made sure of all that He was. Their questions reached at Him like begging fingers.

Thomas said: "Lord, we do not know where You are going. How can we know the way?"

Jesus answered: "I am the way—the truth and the life. No man comes to the Father, but by Me."

Philip leaned over the low table. "Lord, show us the Father, and it is enough for us."

Jesus said: "Have I been with you so long a time and have you not known Me? Philip, he that sees Me sees the Father also. . . . Do you not believe that I am in the Father, and the Father in Me? . . . Yet a little while, and the world sees Me no more. But you see Me, *because I live*—and you shall live.

"In that day you shall know that I am in My Father, and you in Me, and I in you."

Silence lay over that room like the silence of the inmost part of the Temple. A dining table, and twelve men, with one emptied place, the cushion where Judas had reclined.

What He had said was more than they could understand. Their minds touched it and backed away. The words were simple. But the surge of their souls was not.

Jude, from his place beside his brother James, said quietly:

"Lord, how is it that You will manifest Yourself to *us*—and not to the world?"

"If *anyone* love Me," said Jesus, "he will keep My word, and My Father will love him. And We will come to him and will make Our abode with him."

And it was in that hour, that last fragment of time before His going, when never before had men been so intimately united to God, that Jesus told the last parable of His life.

"I am the true vine," He said.

And from their short years with Him echoes leaped: *I am the bread of life,* He had said. *I am the light of the world. I am the door. I am the good shepherd. I am the resurrection and the life. I am the way, the truth, and the life.*

And now He said: "I am the true vine. And My Father is the husbandman.

"Every branch in Me that does not bear fruit He will take away. And every one that bears fruit He will purge it, that it may bring forth more fruit."

They knew the ways of grapes and vineyards, these disciples. They knew the husbandry of the farmer who must destroy the barren deadwood branches and prune the good branches to force them to greater growth.

But they did not begin to see what He meant.

"Abide in Me, and I in you," said Jesus. "As the branch cannot bear fruit of itself, unless it abides in the vine, so neither can you unless you abide in Me."

He waited an instant, as candlelight danced on the chalice from which they had drunk.

"I am the vine," He said. "And you are the branches.

"He that abides in Me and I in him shall bear much fruit. For without Me you can do nothing.

"If anyone abide not in Me, he shall be cast out like a

branch, and shall wither, and they shall gather him up and throw him into the fire, and he burns. . . .

"In this is My Father glorified—that you bring forth very much fruit and become My disciples. As the Father has loved Me, I also love you. Abide in My love."

The vine and its branches. The parable was clear, as simple as bread on the tongue, as infinite and overwhelming as the Son of God Himself.

He was saying that they must live in Him and He in them —with one life, in a union closer than man could dare imagine, as part of Him.

He had spoken to them before of His love for them. He had called them sheep, beloved by the Shepherd Who tended them. He had called them His servants, His guests at the feast, soldiers, hidden leaven, His debtors, sons of His Father. Always in His parables He had stood apart from them, above them. And that had been, they thought, as it should be, as it must be between the Son of God and men.

And now . . . now He stood offering His life not only for them but to them, in the majestic surrender of divine love.

The truth was there in that parable of a vine, the ultimate expression of all that Jesus was. He had come to earth to make men part of Him, to quicken their souls with a new life, a life opening heaven in the embrace of grace.

The truth was that every soul who loved God and His Son, who kept the commandments and lived with God, would live in Him, closer than breath to the body. Every Christian would be a branch of the living Christ, acting, willing, loving, living, dying, suffering, triumphing as one with Him.

And every soul not joined to Him would be dead, withered like a rootless branch, to be swept into the fire. Either you were all His or your soul was without life.

They did not see how it could be. The truth seemed literally too great to be true. But they kept that parable in their hearts. It was like a treasure in a chest for which they did not yet have the key.

The morning would come when the meaning leaped like lifeblood in their souls. The truth of the parable would be opened, after the resurrection, in the fierce splendor of the day when the Holy Spirit came in tongues of fire to make His abode in them. Paul would take that parable and draw from it the glorious truth of the living mystical body of Christ. And in all centuries to come men abiding in Him would explore the science of that life, the stirring theology of the new testament for which He shed His blood.

There would be days of pruning, days of persecution and desolation when the Father would cut back the lush exuberance of faith that wasted itself in leaves instead of fruit. The branches that were unable to bear fruit would be removed. And those that had not the life of the true vine would wither and die and be gathered into the fire. But what remained with the vine would be sturdy and staunch, reaching from heaven to earth.

Already the first had withered. Judas was gone, with death in his soul, on his errand in the night.

Eleven remained, in the first communion between God and man, the beginning of a life that would never end.

It was a farewell dinner. It was also the dawn of a new world.